CONTENTS

INTRODUCTION

This report summarizes mineral resource information for 30 Indian reservations and rancherias in Southern California (Figure 1). It was prepared for the U.S. Bureau of Indian Affairs by the U.S. Bureau of Mines (USBM) and the U.S. Geological Survey (USGS) under an interagency agreement to compile and summarize available information on the geology, minerals, energy resources, and potential for economic development of certain Indian lands. Sources of information are published and unpublished reports, the Mineral Industry Location System (MILS) files of the U.S. Bureau of Mines, and personal communications. Information on the size, population, location, and climate of the reservations was extracted from U.S. Department of Commerce publication (1974). Reports on the water resources of certain reservations have been prepared separately by the U.S. Geological Survey and are available as open file reports from that agency. No fieldwork was carried out on any of the reservations.

ACKNOWLEDGMENTS

Gary Galloway and Roger Hughes of the U.S. Bureau of Mines contributed significantly to the preparation of this report. Mr. Gianelli of the Bureau of Indian Affairs office in Riverside, California, provided current information on the status of Indian lands.

PALA INDIAN RESERVATION

Location

The Pala Indian Reservation is in portions of T. 9 and 10 S., and R. 1 and 2 W., S.B.M., in San Diego County, California (Figure 2). The reservation includes part of the former Mission Indian Reserve and has a total area of approximately 11,488 acres (U.S. Bureau of Indian Affairs, personal communication, 1979). Tribal headquarters is on the reservation at Pala, California, and can be reached via State Highway 76 from Oceanside, 25 miles to the south (Figure 1). Resident population in March 1971 was 255 (U.S. Department of Commerce, 1974).

The reservation lies within the Peninsular Ranges geographic province, and has a terrain characterized by mountains with elevations between 2,000 and 3,700 ft, and by steep-sided canyons with broad alluvial fans at their extremities. The San Luis Rey River crosses the central portion of the reservation and dissects a number of the alluvial fans. Maximum relief is near 3,300 ft. Excellent access to the Pala mining district situated in the northwestern part of the reservation is provided by numerous dirt roads and trails. Access to the southern and eastern parts of the reservation is fair to poor.

Geology

The Pala Indian Reservation is underlain by mostly granitic rocks of the Southern California batholith with local septa of pre-batholithic metamorphic rocks (Figure 3). Alluvium underlies the valley area.

Metamorphic rocks consist of thin septa of schist, quartzite, metasandstone, and meta-conglomerate at several places along the north-western part of the reservation, where they separate batholithic rock of granodioritic composition to the north from gabbroic composition rock to the south (Jahns and Wright, 1951). Metamorphic rock south of the San Luis Rey River and in the northeastern part of the reservation are predominantly well-layered biotite schist and gneiss. Most of this rock consists of alternating layers of biotite-rich and biotite-poor rock. Masses of hornblende-bearing schist occur locally.

Plutonic rocks of the Southern California batholith consist mainly of gabbro, granodiorite-tonalite, and granitic pegmatite dikes. The gabbro, generally named the San Marcos gabbro, is rela-tively resistant to erosion and commonly forms some of the higher hills whose surfaces are man-tled with a dark reddish-brown soil. Most of the gabbro in the Pala area is a relatively homoge-neous, massive, very dark gray olivine-hornblende-hypersthene gabbro. Other Southern California batholithic rocks are distinctly lighter in color than the gabbro.

Granite rocks of tonalite and granodioritic composition occur around the gabbro. Grano-diorite, commonly termed Woodson Mountain granodiorite, predominates in the north and tonalite, commonly termed the Bonsall tonalite, to the south of the San Luis Rey River.

Bonsall tonalite is mainly a medium-grained, gray, massive to foliated biotite-hornblende tonalite with common dark-gray elongate inclu-sions. Woodson Mountain granodiorite is a rela-tively uniform-appearing, massive, coarse-grained biotite granodiorite. Relatively resistant to erosion, it forms pronounced boulder-covered slopes.

Granitic composition pegmatite dikes, repre-senting a younger intrusive part of the Southern California batholith, abound in the Pala area, but are essentially restricted to the gabbro. They are concentrated in an elongate area extending from Pala Canyon northwest of the reservation southeast to Pala Mountain. Most known dikes of commer-cial interest occur north of the San Luis Rey River.

The Pala pegmatites are discrete composi-tionally zoned dikes, mainly striking to the north-west and dipping at low to moderate angles west-ward (Jahns and Wright, 1951). Most dikes are 1 to 3 m in thickness.

The outer parts of these zoned pegmatites consist generally of a medium- to coarse-grained outer zone consisting of quartz, perthite, and plagioclase, with some biotite and with or without biotite, muscovite schorl (black tourmaline), and garnet. Inward, the grain size increases and biotite content decreases. In the thicker dikes, the grain size commonly attains giant-size dimensions in the inner parts of the pegmatite. Intermediate zones between the wall and core in the larger dike can contain a wide variety of unusual minerals. In the Pala district, these include a wide variety of bis-muth minerals, columbite-tantalite, phosphate minerals, and lithium minerals (amblygonite, lepidolite, and spodumene). Pockets within the core zone can contain specimen- and gem-quality tourmaline, spodumene (kunzite), beryl, quartz albite (cleavelandite), and lepidolite. Most of the gem pockets appear to be located in pods or lenses where there is a flattening or roll in the dip of the pegmatite.

Unconsolidated alluvial deposits underlie the valley area. These take the form of coarse bouldery alluvium constituting alluvial fans adjacent to the hills both north and south of the San Luis Rey River and sandy alluvium along the river bottom.

The seismically active Elsinore fault zone diagonally crosses the central part of the reservation. This fault zone consists of a wide main zone of brecciated rock and a number of subparallel faults.

Mineral Resources

The eastern part of the Pala Indian Reservation (T. 9 S., R. 1 W.) was investigated by Irwin and others (1970) during a study of the Agua Tibia Primitive Area, located north of the reservation. Results of geochemical and geophysical surveys indicate that no concealed mineral deposits of commercial size are likely to be present in the study area (Irwin and others, 1970). The authors report the occurrence of thin pegmatite dikes and subeconomic deposits of dimension stone within or adjacent to tribal land.

The southwestern part of the reservation (T. 10 S., R. 2 W.) is largely underlain by gabbroic rock that contains many gem-bearing pegmatites. Little commercial production is reported from these deposits (Jahns and Wright, 1951). The Pala mining district encompasses the major portion of the northwestern part of the reservation (Figure 4).

Pegmatites of the Pala Mining District

The Pala district was the primary source of lithium in the United States during the early part of this century, and is still world-renowned as a source of gemstones and superb mineral specimens. Mining operations began in the 1890's and reached highest production levels from 1900 to 1926, and from 1947 to present (Jahns, 1979). Total district production from 1900 to 1947 exceeded $750,000 and included 23,480 t of lepidolite (lithium mica), 2,980 lb of tourmaline, 1,325 lb of gem spodumene, and small quantities of amblygonite (lithium-aluminum phosphate), beryl, feldspar, and quartz (Jahns and Wright, 1951). These production figures must be considered minimum values because mining records are incomplete or not available, and the amount of material removed by amateur collectors and highgraders is unknown. Production records are not available for the period 1947 to present, although Weber (1963) reported that about 450 lb of gem spodumene was mined from the San Pedro and Vanderburg Mines on Heriot Mountain during the early 1950's. Most of the production from the Pala district has come from six mines, although nearly 100 prospects within the district have been mined on a small scale. Weber (1963, p. 98-115) describes in detail the location, ownership, and geology of the larger prospects.

Lithium ore and gem minerals occur in pegmatite dikes of granitic composition that, with few exceptions, are confined to plutons of gabbroic rocks and mafic tonalites (Jahns, 1979; Jahns and Wright, 1951). The pegmatite dikes are uniformly tabular masses that typically have northerly trends and gentle to moderate westerly dips. They range in thickness from small stringers less than an inch wide, to large dikes with bulges nearly 100 ft across. Most dikes of commercial interest are 5 to 25 ft thick, and can be traced along strike for distances of half a mile or more. Detailed descriptions of the structure, composition, and zoning in the pegmatites may be found in Jahns (1979) and Jahns and Wright (1951).

At least 400 pegmatite dikes are exposed in an area of about 13 mi in the Pala district. Most of the deposits of known commercial interest are on the slopes and crests of Queen, Chief, Little Chief, and Heriot Mountains (Figure 4). The Stewart, Pala Chief, and Katerina pegmatites have been the principal producers of commercial lithium ore in the form of lepidolite and associated spodumene and amblygonite. Some commercial grade feldspar has been produced from the Stewart Mine (Jahns and Wright, 1951). Commercial production of gem-quality tourmaline has been mainly from the Tourmaline King, Tourmaline Queen, Stewart, and Pala Chief pegmatites. Kunzite, a pink gem-quality variety of spodumene, was discovered and mined from pegmatites on Heriot and Chief Mountains. Gem quality beryl and other less abundant gem minerals have been produced sporadically on a small scale from numerous pegmatites in the district. The six mines accounting for most of the production from the Pala district are described in more detail in the following section.

Tourmaline King Mine

The Tourmaline King Mine is in the center of the SE¼ sec. 15, T. 9 S., R. 2 W., on the northwest slope of Queen Mountain, and 1,500 ft north of the Pala Reservation (Figure 4). Surface cuts and more than 1,200 ft of underground workings follow a northwest-trending pegmatite dike. Maximum thickness of the dike is about 16 ft, and its core zone is very discontinuous and poorly defined. The most notable concentration of tourmaline and lepidolite occurred in a discoidal body of pocket pegmatite several tens of feet long, up to 6 ft thick, and at least 30 ft in maximum downdip extent. This body was mined out, and the results of further prospecting suggest that the pegmatite does not offer great promise for future development (Jahns and Wright, 1951).

Tourmaline Queen Mine

The Tourmaline Queen Mine is in the E½SE¼ sec. 15 and SW¼SW¼ sec. 14, T. 9 S., R. 2 W., about 1,500 ft east of the Tourmaline King Mine, and 1,000 ft north of the Pala Reservation (Figure 4). Mine workings consist of two large surface cuts and extensive drifts, inclines, and rooms in the northern part of a pegmatite dike that has a length of at least 3,000 ft and a maximum width of 18 ft. Between 1904 and 1914, this mine was the leading producer of gem tourmaline from the Pala district. Total production from the mine was large, but accurate records are unavailable. Jahns and Wright (1951) reported recorded sales of gem tourmaline amounting to $48,000 for one year. Additional pockets of gem minerals probably are present both adjacent to and downdip from existing underground workings (Jahns and Wright, 1951).

Gem Star Mine

The Gem Star Mine is in the NE¼NW¼ sec. 23, T. 9 S., R. 2 W., on the east slope of Queen Mountain, and within the boundaries of the Pala Reservation. Mine workings consist of numerous surface cuts, inclines, and drifts in the northern extension of the Stewart pegmatite dike. Mining activity was largely restricted to a dike, 15 to 25 ft thick, that comprises the central part of a thick composite intrusion with an outcrop width of 100 to 150 ft. The mine was operated chiefly between 1905 and 1912, producing large quantities of quartz crystal and smaller amounts of lepidolite and gem tourmaline. The pocket pegmatite is fairly continuous and contains gem-quality tourmaline crystals, as much as 4 in. in diameter and 15 in. in length, associated with lepidolite, smoky quartz, albite, rare spodumene, and pink clay. Similar material probably remains to be mined, although quantities of gem-quality crystals may be limited (Jahns and Wright, 1951).

Stewart Mine

The Stewart Mine, once the largest producer of lithium in the United States, is in the SE¼NW¼ sec. 23, T. 9 S., R. 2 W., on the Pala Reservation. Mine workings consist of large, open cuts, several adits and inclines, and numerous drifts in the southern end of the Stewart dike, which is at least 80 ft thick throughout much of the mine area. The internal structure and zoning of the dike in the mine area are very complex (Figure 5). A quartz-spodumene pegmatite forms lensoidal masses as much as 150 ft long and 15 ft thick in the core of the dike. Most of the lepidolite-rich pegmatite is in the footwall part of the central zone.

Lepidolite was mined from two principal orebodies along or near a bench-like roll in the dike (Figure 5), both measuring about 200 ft long, 20 to 180 ft wide, and averaging 10 ft thick. Additional large lenses of lepidolite-rich pegmatite may be present in the dike, either along strike north of the present mine workings, or downdip (Jahns and Wright, 1951).

The mine was active between 1892 and 1907, and again between 1914 and 1928, producing lepidolite and small quantities of amblygonite, gem tourmaline, and beryl. Total output reported between 1892 and 1928 was about 22,500 t of lepidolite and amblygonite that averaged 3 to 4 percent lithium oxide (Weber, 1963). Jahns and Wright (1951) reported that an irregular mass of native bismuth weighing more than 100 lb was encountered in the underground workings not far from the west adit.

The bismuth occurred as long, irregular crystals, and platy crystalline masses up to 15 mm long, and was associated with quartz, spodumene, and amblygonite (Kunz, 1903).

In 1968, the mine was reopened by Pala Properties International, the present operators of the mine. Several new inclines and drifts were opened, which yielded approximately 650 lb of gem- and specimen-grade tourmaline during the period 1968 to 1973 (Jahns, 1979). Descriptions of tourmaline produced during this period may be found in Sinkankas (1976).

Pala Chief Mine

The Pala Chief Mine is in the SE¼SE¼ sec. 14, T. 9 S., R. 2 W., near the summit of Chief Mountain, several hundred feet north of the reservation (Figure 4). The main pegmatite mass is a northwest-trending dike complex, at least 3,200 ft long and 16 to 36 ft thick. The core of the dike consists of discoidal masses of quartz-spodumene pegmatite with pockets that contain lepidolite, tourmaline, quartz, spodumene, and beryl. The mine was operated most intensively from 1903 to 1918 and was considered the world's foremost source of gem spodumene. Excellent gem-quality spodumene occurs near the surface to the south of the main open cut; additional gem-bearing material probably exists down the dip of the dike (Jahns and Wright, 1951).

Katerina Mine

The Katerina Mine is in the SW¼SE¼ sec. 24, T. 9 S., R. 2 W., on the southwestern slope of Heriot Mountain and within the Pala Reservation. The mine workings consist of numerous open cuts, tunnels, and inclines, which extend for 640 ft along a thick, continuous dike complex. Individual dikes in the complex range in thickness from a few inches to 32 ft. The main orebody is located in a quartz-spodumene mass, at least 85 ft long by 70 ft wide by 8 ft thick, that forms the core of a large bulge in the middle dike. The deposit has produced substantial quantities of lepidolite, gem spodumene, quartz, and beryl, and is one of the chief sources of unusual minerals in the district. Exploration down the dip of the dike will probably reveal appreciable quantities of gem material. Other parts of the general dike complex contain evidence of lepidolite, spodumene, and beryl mineralization and warrant further prospecting (Jahns and Wright, 1951).

Dimension Stone

Dimension stone has been mined from the Magee Quarry in the SE¼ sec. 19, T. 9 S., R. 1 W., just outside reservation boundaries (Figure 2). The stone produced is a variety of gabbro that is referred to commercially as "black granite" and has been used mainly for monuments and facing stone. Irwin and others (1970) reported that the quarry was in operation during their reconnaissance, and has produced a few tens of thousands of tons. The "black granite" is quarried from the San Marcos gabbro, which occurs in irregular bodies as much as several miles in maximum surface dimension throughout much of San Diego County, including parts of the Pala Reservation (Weber, 1963).

Sand and Gravel

Royalties received from San Diego Consolidated Sand and Gravel, Inc., for a lease on a sand and gravel operation provide the principal source of tribal income. The quarry is in an alluvial fan deposit in the NE¼ sec. 26, T. 9 S., R. 2 W. (Figure 2). The deposit covers an area of about ¼ mi to a depth of at least 20 ft and consists of crudely stratified lenses of cobbles and boulders, with numerous cobbles exceeding 6 in. in diameter and occasional boulders measuring 3 to 6 ft across. After being crushed, sized, and washed, the material is used as concrete aggregate and in the production of asphalt (Goldman, 1968).

Recommendations for Further Work

The Pala mining district, which lies largely within the Pala Reservation, was one of the most productive pegmatite mining regions in the United States during the first half of this century, and is still a major source of gemstones and rare minerals. The principal source of lithium today is spodumene ore mined from pegmatites in North Carolina, which has total estimated reserves of about 300,000 t of lithium equivalent (Singleton, 1979). Increased use of lithium in aluminum reduction cells, breeder reactors, and batteries suggests a conservative four-fold increase in United States demand by the year 2000. A sharper increase in demand, due to extensive use of rechargeable batteries in motor vehicles or to newly discovered uses for lithium, could possibly make lithium production from the Pala district economically feasible if new orebodies are located.

In view of this possibility, as well as the present high prices for gemstones and mineral specimens and the current mining activity in the pegmatites of the region, a thorough evaluation of pegmatite reserves on tribal lands is strongly recommended. Exposures in several mines suggest additional reserves of gem-bearing material, and numerous prospects appear favorable. The most promising untested exploration targets are large pegmatite dikes that contain units rich in coarse, anhedral quartz. The exploration program should include the Pala mining district and the southern portion of the reservation where large pegmatite-

bearing gabbroic bodies occur. The Pala band would also benefit from an evaluation of potential resources of dimension stone and any associated metallic minerals.

PAUMA AND YUIMA INDIAN RESERVATION

Location

The Pauma and Yuima Indian Reservation, situated in portions of T. 9 and 10 S., R. 1 W., S.B.M., San Diego County, California (Figure 6), includes part of the former Mission Indian Reserve and has a total area of approximately 5,877 acres (U.S. Bureau of Indian Affairs, personal commun., 1979). Tribal headquarters is at Pauma Valley and can be reached via State Highway 76 from Oceanside, 25 mi to the southwest. Portions of the west boundary of the reservation adjoin the Pala Indian Reservation. In 1971, 59 Indians resided on or adjacent to the reservation.

The reservation lies almost entirely in a mountainous area with elevations ranging from less than 1,000 ft to over 5,000 ft. The climate is moderate, with an average annual rainfall of about 24 in. Access is generally poor throughout most of the reservation.

Geology

Mineral Resources

The area which presently makes up the greater part of the Pauma and Yuima Indian Reservation was examined in 1969 by the U. S. Geological

Survey and the U.S. Bureau of Mines as part of an evaluation of the mineral potential of the Agua Tibia Primitive Area (Irwin and others, 1970). No economic mineral deposits were found and analyses of more than 100 stream-sediment and bedrock samples collected adjacent to the primitive area indicate the absence of geochemical anomalies commonly associated with economic mineral deposits. No prospect pits or mines were seen during the examination and a search of courthouse records revealed no past or present mining claims in the area.

Based on the report by Irwin and others (1970), it would appear the mineral potential on the Pauma and Yuima Indian Reservation is low. The Pala mining district, located about 3 mi west of the reservation boundary, is a long-standing source of pegmatite minerals (see section on Pala Indian Reservation). However, economic pegmatite bodies have not been reported on the Pauma and Yuima Reservation.

The main parcel of the Pauma Indian Reservation is underlain by nearly equal amounts of pre-Southern California batholith schist and gneiss and granitic rock of the batholith (Figure 7). The schist and gneiss are predominantly well-layered biotite-rich rocks consisting mostly of alternate layers of biotite-rich and biotite-poor rock. Locally, there are masses of hornblende-bearing schist.

Granitic rock consists mainly of biotite-granodiorite and biotite- hornblende tonalite similar to that which underlies the northern part of the Pala Reservation immediately to the west.

The smaller parcel of the Pauma Indian Reservation and the two small parcels which comprise

the Yuima Indian Reservation (Figure 8) are underlain by bouldery alluvial fan alluvium.

Parts of the reservation are crossed by or are adjacent to faults related to the seismically active Elsinore fault zone.

PECHANGA INDIAN RESERVATION

Location

The Pechanga Indian Reservation, situated in T. 8 S., R. 2 W., S.B.M., Riverside County, California (Figure 9), has a total area of 4,097 acres and a population of about 21 Indians. Tribal headquarters is in Temecula, California.

The reservation is on low-lying terrain dissected by numerous stream drainages. Elevations are between about 1,100 and 2,700 ft; access is good throughout the reservation.

Geology

The Pechanga Indian Reservation is underlain by a mixture of plutonic rocks and nonmarine sedimentary rocks of late Tertiary and Quaternary age (Figure 10). Plutonic rocks, part of the Southern California batholith of Cretaceous age, underlie the eastern and southern parts of the larger reservation parcel and the southwestern part of the smaller parcel. The plutonic rocks include gabbro, granodiorite, and quartz-monzonite (Kennedy, 1977). The gabbro, generally termed the San Marcos gabbro, consists of primarily a coarse-grained nearly black hornblende gabbro with lesser amounts of pyroxene and olivine gabbro. It weathers to form a reddish brown soil studded with small dark boulders of disintegration. The granodiorite and quartz-monzonite are light-gray coarse-grained massive-appearing biotite and biotite-hornblende-bearing rocks. They commonly weather to form large gray boulders of disintegration. The soil derived from these rocks is mainly grayish, in contrast to the red-brown soil derived from gabbro.

Unconformably overlying the batholithic rocks are sediments of Pliocene age, termed the Temecula Arkose (Mann, 1955; Kennedy, 1977). These sediments are best exposed along Pechanga Creek. This unit takes its name from nearby Temecula; however, the Temecula Arkose underlies most of the larger reservation parcel. It consists of greenish-yellow, moderately well-indurated, medium-bedded, medium- to coarse-grained arkosic sandstone with lesser amounts of siltstone, claystone, and discontinuous conglomeratic beds.

Overlying the Temecula Arkose in the southwestern part of the larger reservation parcel and resting on quartz-monzonite in the smaller parcel is a late Pleistocene sedimentary unit, the Pauba Formation (Kennedy, 1977), named after nearby Rancho Pauba. This unit consists of light-brown, moderately well-indurated sandstone with siltstone and discontinuous conglomeratic beds.

Younger than, and overlying the Temecula Arkose in the southwestern part of the larger reservation parcel, is the Dripping Springs Formation (Mann, 1955; Kennedy, 1977). This sedimentary unit consists of a brownish, poorly consolidated pebble-to-boulder fanglomerate. The clasts are of local origin.

Late Quaternary stream-terrace deposits occur locally along Pechanga Creek. These consist of brownish, well-indurated, coarse-grained sand and conglomerate. The youngest Holocene-age deposits consist of unconsolidated grayish alluvium which occurs along Pechanga Creek.

The reservation is crossed by numerous strands of the active, complex Elsinore fault zone. Surface expression of faulting is best exposed in the western part of the larger reservation parcel, where there are a number of closed depressions along several of the faults. Fault displacements along the Elsinore fault are considered to be largely right-lateral strike-slip.

Mineral Resources

No mines or mineral deposits are known to exist on the reservation. Sand and gravel in the stream bed of Pechanga Creek are probably adequate for local use. Gem-quality tourmaline, lepidolite, and dimension stone have been mined from pegmatite dikes in the Pala district, 4 mi to the south (Jahns and Wright, 1951). Regional geology suggests that similar dikes may occur on the extreme southern and eastern edges of the reservation, but none have been reported in the literature. A reconnaissance study of the mineral resources of the Agua Tibia Primitive Area, immediately east and southeast of the reservation, disclosed no evidence of significant metallic or nonmetallic mineral deposits (Irwin and others, 1970).

RINCON INDIAN RESERVATION

Location

The Rincon Indian Reservation, situated in portions of T. 10 and 11 S., R. 1 W., S.B.M., San Diego County, California (Figure 11), comprises a total of 3,975 acres in the lower end of Pauma Valley (Valley of the San Luis Rey River) and the mountainous area on either side of the valley. Elevations range from about 840 ft on the valley floor to about 2,300 ft in the brush-covered mountains.

Access to the reservation is via paved County Highway 6. San Diego is 45 mi away and Escondido 17 mi by paved highway. Climate is mild, and annual rainfall averages about 20 in (Ellis and Lee, 1919, plate XV). In 1972, 91 Indians resided on or adjacent to the reservation.

Geology

Basement rock underlying the Rincon Indian Reservation consists of tonalite cut by granitic pegmatite dikes, both part of the Southern California batholith of Cretaceous age (Figure 12). The tonalite, generally termed Bonsall tonalite, is a massive to foliated coarse-grained granitic rock which commonly weathers to give rise to slopes with scattered boulders and ledges of low relief. Mineralogically, this rock is a biotite-hornblende tonalite. A swarm of granitic-composition pegmatite dikes cut this tonalite. Most of these dikes occur north and east of the San Luis Rey River, where they weather to form a series of pronounced low ribs above the more readily weathered tonalite.

These dikes strike north to northwest and dip at moderate angles to the west. Mineralogically, most of these dikes consist of quartz and feldspar, with biotite and muscovite in common but minor amounts. Most dikes are compositionally zoned with an outer zone consisting of coarse-grained biotite, muscovite, quartz, and feldspar. Intermediate zones, present in only a few pegmatites, consist of feldspar, quartz, and muscovite, with minor amounts of beryl, tourmaline, and garnet. Core zones consist of mainly quartz and feldspar with sparse and very local occurrences of beryl, columbite, cassiterite, bismuth minerals, spodumene (kunzite), lepidolite, amblygonite, petalite, and helvite. Quartz crystals were obtained commercially from one pegmatite in the district in the 1940's.

Coarse bouldery alluvium occurs along the flanks of the hills and gray sandy alluvium occurs in Paradise Creek and San Luis Rey River.

Mineral Resources

A number of small prospect pits are present in pegmatite dikes on the Rincon Indian Reservation (Figure 11). The Rincon pegmatites are similar to those in the nearby Pala district (Hanley, 1951). Most of these pegmatites are mineralogically simple and contain essential quartz, perthite, and plagioclase and subordinate muscovite. A few contain schorl, beryl, and garnet as accessory minerals; very few of the pegmatites are lithiabearing. The mineralogy of the pegmatites has been described by Kunz (1905), Waring (1905), Ford (1906), Rogers (1910), and Murdoch and Webb (1948). Generally striking N. 25° W., and dipping about 45° SW., the pegmatite dikes appear to have been intruded along regional joints in the San Marcos gabbro and Bonsall tonalite bodies.

The Mack Mine is just off the reservation in the SW¼SW¼ sec. 25, T. 10 S., R. 1 W., S.B.M. (Figure 11). Mine workings consist of a series of three open cuts, the largest 61 ft long, 32 ft wide, and 16 ft deep. The mine was worked shortly after the turn of the century and produced small quantities of beryl crystals, some of which were transparent aquamarines of gem quality (Hanley, 1951).

The Victor Mine is in the SE¼NW¼ sec. 36, T. 10 S., R. 1 W., on the west slope of Mack Ridge, less than half a mile east of the reservation boundary. A small open cut and short underground workings explore a quartz-albite-muscovite pegmatite. Hanley (1951) described the deposit in some detail and concluded that it has been essentially mined out.

The Clark Mine is in the NE¼SW¼ sec. 36, T. 10 S., R. 1 W., a short distance south of the Victor Mine (Figure 11). Workings consist of a series of small open cuts and two small adits (Hanley, 1951). During World War II, the mine produced a few tens of pounds of quartz crystals for use in oscillator plates (Hanley, 1951; Weber, 1963).

Hanley (1951) reported that the Rincon pegmatites have little economic value except as possible sources of gemstones and feldspar. Mining activity was greatest in the early 1900's at the time the Chinese were buying American semiprecious stones for carving. Domestic interest in these deposits subsequently decreased. However, the present increased demand for semiprecious stones and mineral specimens warrants a detailed reexamination of the Rincon pegmatites.

LA JOLLA INDIAN RESERVATION

Location

The La Jolla Indian Reservation is in the southern portion of T. 10 S., R. 1 E., S.B.M., San Diego County, California (Figure 13). State Highway 76 runs east-west through the reservation and provides access to Escondido, 25 mi to the southwest. In 1971, 23 Indians lived on or adjacent to the reservation.

The reservation consists of a total of 8,233 acres, of which 7,279 acres are tribally owned; the remainder, mostly agricultural land, is allotted (U.S. Department of Commerce, 1974). Annual rainfall ranges from 20 in. in the western part of the reservation to around 30 in. in the eastern part (Ellis and Lee, 1919, plate XV). Elevations range from less than 1,000 ft in the valley of the San Luis Rey River to over 5,000 ft in the northeast corner of the reservation. Most of the reservation is mountainous country covered with a thick growth of brush.

Geology

The La Jolla Indian Reservation is underlain by granitic rocks of the Cretaceous-age Southern California batholith and a lesser amount of prebatholith schist (Figure 14). The westernmost part of the reservation is underlain by the eastward continuation of tonalite (Bonsall tonalite) underlying the Rincon Reservation, which includes numerous granitic pegmatite dikes. This tonalite is a massive to foliated, coarse-grained, biotite-hornblende tonalite, which weathers to give rise to slopes with scattered boulders and ledges of low relief. East of the pegmatite-bearing Bonsall tonalite is the northern part of a pluton comprised of granodiorite, commonly termed the Woodson Mountain granodiorite. This rock is a relatively uniform, massive, coarse-grained biotite-granodiorite. East of the Woodson Mountain granodiorite is a complex assemblage of pre-batholithic schist and gneiss and batholithic rocks ranging from gabbro to granodiorite in composition, crossed by the northwest-striking Elsinore faut zone.

Discontinuous, flat-lying Quaternary-age bouldery alluvial deposits occur along the San Luis Rey River. Brecciated basement rock and coarse bouldery alluvial fan deposits occur along the north side of Highway 76.

The center of the reservation is crossed by the seismically active northwest-striking Elsinore fault zone. The fault zone here consists of a poorly exposed thick brecciated rock zone as much as 2,000 ft in width.

Mineral Resources

The only mineral deposit on the La Jolla Indian Reservation reported in the literature is the Calac Prospect situated near the center S½ sec. 19, T. 10 S., R. 1 E., S.B.M. (Figure 13). The prospect consists of five small pits in two pegmatite dikes that strike about N. 40° W., dip about 15° SW., and crop out continuously for several thousand feet (Hanley, 1951). The northern dike varies in thickness from 3 to 4 ft; quartz-perthite pods in the central part range in thickness from 2 to 12 in. and some contain sparse beryl around their margins.

The southern dike averages about 3½ ft thick and contains a quartz-perthite core. Bright blue, greenish-blue, and yellowish-green beryl crystals as much as 13 mm in diameter occur in the core of the dike, on its margins, and above it in graphic granite (Hanley, 1951). Production from the prospect has been small (Weber, 1963).

Hanley (1951) concluded the northern dike probably is not economically favorable for mining of beryl. The southern dike contains a greater percentage of gem-quality beryl and may be more favorable for development. With the increased interest during the past several years in semiprecious gemstones, it would be worthwhile to reevaluate the Calac Prospect as well as other gembearing dikes exposed in the area.

No gold deposits are reported in the literature either on or near the La Jolla Indian Reservation, although rock types on the reservation are similar to those hosting gold deposits in other areas in San Diego County. A reconnaissance sampling program should be carried out to determine if gold or other metals occur on the reservation.

SAN PASQUAL INDIAN RESERVATION

Location

The San Pasqual Indian Reservation occupies portions of seven sections in T. 11 S., R. 1 W., S.B.M., San Diego County, California (Figure 15). The total area of the reservation is approximately 1,380 acres, and the resident population is about 19. Tribal headquarters is in Valley Center, California, and the nearest sizable town is Escondido, about 10 mi to the southwest. Elevations on the reservation range between 1,500 and 2,300 ft; nearly all the land is mountainous and covered with brush. Annual average rainfall is about 20 in. (Ellis and Lee, 1919, pl. 15).

Geology

The San Pasqual Indian Reservation is underlain by granitic rocks of the Cretaceous-age Southern California batholith, with a small septum of pre-batholithic schist in the west-central part of the reservation (Figure 16). The schist consists of an east-oriented elongate mass of layered biotite schist and gneiss. The granitic rock ranges from granodiorite to tonalite, with a small mass of gabbro, commonly termed the San Marcos gabbro, in the southernmost part of the Reservation.

Flat-lying unconsolidated Holocene alluvium underlies Woods Valley. Margins of this alluvium-floored valley extend into parts of the reservation.

Mineral Resources

Neither the published literature nor the files of the U.S. Bureau of Mines indicate the existence of any mineral deposits on the San Pasqual Indian Reservation. Rock types on the reservation are similar to those in which deposits of both metallic and nonmetallic minerals occur elsewhere in San Diego County (Weber, 1963). The only deposits reported near the reservation are the Haldredge quartz deposit and the Langer feldspar deposit (Figure 15).

The Haldredge quartz deposit is in the SE¼SE¼ sec. 23, T. 11 S., R. 1 W., S.B.M. It consists of a pegmatite dike about 50 ft long and

15 ft wide that contains rose quartz (Weber, 1963). No development or production has been recorded.

The Langer feldspar deposit is in the SW¼SE¼ sec. 26, T. 11 S., R. 1 W., S.B.M. Weber (1963) described the deposit as a pegmatite dike that strikes N. 15 E., dips steeply west, and is at least 150 ft long and at least 25 ft thick. The dike is composed chiefly of shattered anhedral to subhedral crystals of potash feldspar and quartz as much as several feet in diameter. Mica and other accessory minerals are sparse. The deposit has been developed with a 30 ft adit driven along the strike of the dike. A small amount of feldspar was mined from the deposit in 1928.

According to published reports, mineral potential of the San Pasqual Indian Reservation does not appear encouraging. However, the lack of reported deposits on the reservation may be partly attributed to a lack of exploration within its boundaries. Because potential exists for the occurrence of pegmatite bodies, a reconnaissance study of the area is warranted.

SANTA YSABEL INDIAN RESERVATION

Location

The Santa Ysabel Indian Reservation is situated in portions of T. 11 and 12 S., R. 2 and 3 E., San Diego County, California (Figure 17). The reservation is made up of three separate parcels of land with a total area of 10,000 acres and a resident population of about 106. The town of Ramona, about 16 mi to the southwest, can be reached via State Highway 79. Tribal headquarters is in Santa Ysabel, California.

Elevations on the reservation range between 5,700 and 2,100 ft with moderate to steep local relief. The climate is warm and dry with an average rainfall of about 15 in. per year.

Geology

The Santa Ysabel Indian Reservation is underlain by granitic rocks of the Cretaceous-age Southern California batholith and pre-batholithic schist (Figure 18). Batholithic rock in the northern part of the larger parcel is tonalite, which has been termed the Lakeview Mountain tonalite (Merriam, 1958). It is a massive gray biotite-hornblende tonalite, which commonly weathers to form large boulders. South of the tonalite is a large body of intimately intermingled pre-batholithic metamorphic rock (schist) and granitic rock of the Southern California batholith. The schist and gneiss part of this complex is layered, which is characterized by variable amounts of biotite. In the southern part of the reservation, schist is present without a granitic component.

Unconsolidated Holocene alluvium deposits occur along some of the larger creeks. The northwest-striking seismically active Elsinore fault zone is localized along the western margin of this parcel.

In the northern of the two smaller parcels, mixed granitic rock and schist similar to that in the larger parcels occur, intruded by a body of gabbro. This gabbro, the San Marcos gabbro, is part of the Southern California batholith. Here it forms an elongate west-northwest-oriented pluton. The gabbro is mainly a coarse-grained massive hornblende gabbro which weathers to give rise to a reddish-brown soil studded with cobbles and boulders of unweathered gabbro.

Unconsolidated Holocene alluvium occurs in the valley floor along Scholder Creek in the western part of this parcel.

In the southern of the smaller parcels, pre-batholithic schist and gneiss are the predominant rock types.

Mixed schist and granitic rock of the Southern California batholith occur in the northern and eastern parts of this parcel. Schist and gneiss, generally termed the Julian schist, comprise the bulk of the southwestern part of the parcel. The schist and gneiss are layered rocks with the definition of the layers being produced by variation in the biotite content. Amphibole-bearing schist occurs locally.

Granodiorite of the Southern California batholith occurs in the northwestern part of this parcel. Generally termed Woodson Mountain granodiorite, it is a light-gray, generally massive rock. It commonly weathers to form large boulders.

Mineral Resources

No mineral occurrences are reported within the boundaries of the Santa Ysabel Reservation. Geologic formations that crop out on tribal land are known producers of gold, tungsten, and gemstones in other parts of San Diego County, including areas peripheral to the reservation (Merriam, 1946; Weber, 1963). This suggests that the lack of reported mineral deposits on the reservation may be the result of little or no past exploration. A brief description of nearby mining activity may give some indication of the mineral resource potential of the reservation.

The Shenandoah Gold Mine is north of the reservation boundary in the NW¼ sec. 23, T. 11 S., R. 2 E. (Figure 17). Discovered in the late 1880's, this mine was worked until 1896 and again in 1932. The gold occurs in a quartz vein that is 1 to 2½ ft wide, strikes northeast, and dips northwest. The vein was explored by a 175 ft shaft and several hundred feet of drifts. Weber (1963) estimated past production to be about $50,000 worth of gold (at $20 per ounce). During its period of activity, the property included a 5-stamp mill.

The northwest corner of the reservation adjoins the Mesa Grande gem mining district (Weber, 1963, pl. 4), which has been the most productive of the gem-bearing areas of California. An estimated quarter of a million pounds of tourmaline, valued at nearly $800,000, and smaller amounts of quartz, beryl, and other gem minerals have been produced from the pegmatites of the Mesa Grande district (Wright, 1957).

The Himalaya Mine, with a total output of between 150,000 and 200,000 lb of gem tourmaline and several hundred pounds of gem beryl, has been the most productive gem mine in California and is unsurpassed in the world as a source of gem tourmaline. Other producers in the Mesa Grande district are the Esmeralda, Mesa Grande, Rose Quartz, and San Diego Mines (Weber, 1963). The Himalaya and San Diego Mines are in operation at the present time (Jahns, 1979).

These mines, all within 2 mi of the reservation, occur in geologic formations that are also present on the reservation, thus indicating that examination of the reservation might reveal additional gem-bearing pegmatites and gold-bearing quartz veins. In view of the recent popularity and dramatic increase in value of gold and semiprecious gemstones, it is recommended that a reconnaissance and geochemical sampling program be carried out in geologically favorable areas on the Santa Ysabel Reservation.

MESA GRANDE INDIAN RESERVATION

Location

The Mesa Grande Indian Reservation is in the north-central portion of San Diego County, California, about 10 mi northeast of Ramona. The reservation has a total area of 120 acres in secs. 8 and 9, T. 12 S., R. 2 E., just west of the Santa Ysabel Reservation (Figure 17). Tribal headquarters is in Pala, California, and no persons were living on the reservation in 1972. The reservation is situated principally in Black Canyon; elevations range from 2,000 ft in the stream valley to 2,460 ft on the surrounding hills.

Geology

The Mesa Grande Indian Reservation is underlain by granodiorite, generally termed the Woodson Mountain granodiorite, of the Cretaceous-age Southern California batholith (Figure 18). The granodiorite is a light-gray, massive-appearing biotite or biotite-hornblende granodiorite which commonly weathers to form large boulders.

Thin, bouldery Holocene alluvium occurs along Black Canyon, which is located in the center of the reservation.

Mineral Resources

No mineral deposits are reported within the boundaries of the Mesa Grande Indian Reservation. The small size of the Reservation limits mineral potential, although the geologic formations exposed on the reservation are all favorable host rocks for mineral deposits at other locations in San Diego County.

The Old Ironsides nickel deposit is about 2 mi northwest of the reservation in the NW¼SW¼ sec. 6, T. 12 S., R. 2 E., S.B.M. A nickel-cobalt-copper-bearing gossan in gabbro crops out over an area 325 ft long and 40 to 60 ft wide (Weber, 1963). Exploration of the deposit was carried out in 1954 and consisted of two inclined drill holes, 219 ft and 387 ft deep. Although some nickel-cobalt-copper minerals were intersected, the deposit was not considered to have sufficient economic value to warrant further exploration.

About a mile southwest of the Mesa Grande Indian Reservation in the NW¼ sec. 20, T. 12 S., R. 2 E., S.B.M., the Black Canyon feldspar deposit is exposed along the east side of Black Canyon road. The deposit consists of a pegmatite body containing abundant potash feldspar, quartz, and biotite (Weber, 1963). In the mid-1930's, the mine yielded about 5 t of feldspar but has been inactive since then.

Although the rock formations that occur on the Mesa Grande Indian Reservation are favorable hosts for mineral deposits, the potential for discovery and development of an economic mineral resource is low due to the limited size of the target area. Reconnaissance of the area in conjunction with a survey of the adjacent Santa Ysabel Reservation is warranted.

INAJA-COSMIT INDIAN RANCHERIA

Location

The Inaja-Cosmit Indian Rancheria is situated in portions of secs. 25, 26, and 35, T. 13 S., R. 3 E., San Diego County, California (Figure 19), about 75 mi northeast of San Diego in a mountainous area adjacent to the Cleveland National Forest. Tribal headquarters is in Julian, located about 7 mi northeast of the rancheria at the intersection of State Highways 78 and 79.

The rancheria consists of 880 acres and has a resident population of approximately 10 Indians. Climate on the rancheria is relatively mild with rainfall of about 30 in. per year (Ellis and Lee, 1919). Elevations range from slightly less than 3,000 ft to almost 4,000 ft.

Geology

The Inaja Indian Rancheria is underlain by an intimately mingled mixture of granitic rock of the Cretaceous-age Southern California batholith and pre-batholithic schist and gneiss (Merriam, 1958) (Figure 20). Layering in the schist and gneiss is discontinuous, generally produced by variation in the biotite content. Most of the schist and gneiss is a biotite-feldspar-quartz schist with local hornblende-bearing schist and gneiss. Schist devoid of granitic rock occurs in the southeast corner of the rancheria.

The Cosmit Rancheria is underlain by similar mixed rock in the westernmost part of the rancheria, as in the Inaja Rancheria, and a north-oriented elongate body of mixed rock extending into the south-central part of the rancheria (Merriam, 1958). Between the two bodies of mixed rock is a small body of schist and gneiss, generally termed the Julian schist.

The Julian schist is a biotite-bearing schist consisting of discontinuous layers of variable biotite content. Hornblende-bearing schist occurs locally.

The eastern part of the rancheria is underlain by the San Marcos gabbro of the Cretaceous-age Southern California batholith. The gabbro consists mainly of coarse-grained hornblende gabbro which weathers to form a reddish-brown soil.

Mineral Resources

No mineral occurrences are reported within the boundaries of the Inaja and Cosmit Rancherias. The Boulder Creek gold district lies about 3 mi southwest of the rancherias (Weber, 1963), where mineral deposits occur in gneissic and granitic rocks of Cretaceous age that are similar to rocks cropping out on the rancheria. The principal gold-bearing deposits occur in several northwest-trending mineralized shear zones along the north side of Boulder Creek. Other deposits in the area consist of narrow quartz veins and veinlets in hybrid rocks. Gold was discovered in the district about 1885 and the deposits worked sporadically and on a small scale until the 1920's. However, the district was never a prolific producer, and the gold ore is of very low grade (Weber, 1963).

The well-known gold district of Julian is about 6 mi northeast of the rancherias. Geology of the Julian deposits is similar to that of the Boulder Creek district and has been described in detail by Weber (1963), Ellsberg (1972), Merriam (1958), Creasey (1946), and Donnelly (1934).

BARONA INDIAN RANCHERIA

Location

The Barona Indian Rancheria is in San Diego County, California, about 28 mi northeast of San Diego. Services are available in El Cajon, 12 mi south, and Ramona, about 5 mi north of the rancheria. A paved county road traverses the rancheria longitudinally, providing good access (Figure 21). The rancheria occupies an irregular-shaped area of 5,005 acres in T. 14 S., R. 1 and 2 E., S.B.M., and has a population of about 104. Tribal headquarters is in Lakeside, California.

The rancheria occupies Barona Valley and surrounding hillsides. The land is largely rocky and hilly, with elevations ranging from about 1,300 ft to slightly over 2,000 ft. Access is good through-out.

Geology

All but a small part of the Barona Indian Rancheria is underlain by granitic rocks of the Cretaceous-age Southern California batholith (Weber, 1963) (Figure 22). A small mass of pre-batholithic quartzite occurs in the southern part of the rancheria (sec. 26, T. 14 S., R. 1 E., S.B.M.). This off-white-colored rock consists primarily of quartz with a little feldspar and trace amounts of several other minerals.

The batholithic rock consists primarily of granitic rock of granodioritic and tonalitic composition. Most are light gray biotite and biotite-hornblende-bearing, massive, and weather to form large boulders.

Eocene conglomerate occurs in two localities along the western part of the rancheria. These occurrences are the eastern part of a thick sequence of marine Eocene rocks, termed the Poway Conglomerate in the San Diego area. The conglomerate consists of near-horizontal, indurated, poorly bedded, cobbly conglomerate. The clasts are composed almost entirely of a slightly metamorphosed silicic volcanic rock (welded tuff).

Unconsolidated Holocene grayish alluvium occurs in the central part of Barona Valley.

Mineral Resources

Two known mineral deposits fall within the boundaries of the Barona Indian Rancheria: the Klondike gold deposit and the Featherstone quartzite deposit. Four mineral deposits are reported to be within 2 mi of the rancheria boundaries: the Daley copper mine, the McFall garnet mine, and the El Cajon and Merrill kaolin deposits (Figure 21).

The Klondike gold deposit is in sec. 1, T. 14 S., R. 1 E., S.B.M., within the boundaries of the Barona Rancheria. The U.S. Bureau of Mines MILS system places it within the W½SW¼SE¼ of sec 1, although no reference is given as to the

source of this information and no field check has been made by the Bureau of Mines. Mining activity was reported (Hubon, 1902) to consist of shallow workings in quartz veins within schist country rock, but no trace of activity could be found in 1957 (Weber, 1963).

The Featherstone quartzite deposit is situated in the center of the N½N½ sec. 26, T. 14 S., R. 1 E., S.B.M. The deposit occurs as a pendant in granitic rocks and has outcrop dimensions of about ⅜ mi long and ⅛ mi wide. The quartzite is fine- to medium-grained and is composed chiefly of quartz and sparse feldspar, with minor amounts of garnet, hematite, and other accessory minerals. The deposit was undeveloped in 1957 (Weber, 1963).

The McFall garnet mine is near the center of sec. 5, T. 14 S., R. 2 E., S.B.M., about a mile east of the northeast corner of the reservation. The deposit consists of a small body of garnet- and epidote-bearing tactite adjacent to granitic rocks of Cretaceous age that extend onto the rancheria. The deposit was located in 1895 as a zinc deposit and was explored by a 22 ft shaft (now caved) sunk through a large mass of abrasive-grade garnet (Kunz, 1905). A few years later, the mine was the source of a small amount of gem-quality epidote. The mine was relocated in 1955 and worked briefly for garnet (Weber, 1963).

The Daley copper mine is near the center of sec. 11, T. 14 S., R. 1 E., S.B.M., about ¾ mi west of the western boundary of the rancheria. The deposit was discovered in 1894 and worked from 1915 to about 1923. Ore was smelted in a 50-t reverberatory furnace on the property and produced about 175,000 lb of copper (Weber, 1963). The orebody consisted of a north-trending zone of mineralization, 150 ft long and 50 ft wide, along a contact between granite and schist (Tucker, 1924). A zone of oxidation extended to a depth of 30 ft and consisted of limonite, black copper oxides, malachite, and azurite. Finely divided chalcopyrite, with pyrite, occurs below the oxide zone. The ore averaged 2 to 3 percent copper and 6 oz/t of silver. Workings consist of a 115 ft deep vertical shaft and associated drifts and surface cuts (Weber, 1963).

The El Cajon kaolin deposit is on the west flank of El Cajon Mountain in the NW¼(?) sec. 36, T. 14 S., R. 1 E., S.B.M., about a mile southeast of the southeast corner of the Barona Rancheria (Weber, 1963). Dietrich (1928) reported that from 1914 to 1916 about 400 t of kaolin from the deposit were shipped to the Faience Tile Plant of the former California China Clay Products Company at National City. The deposit was explored by several adits and an open cut during this period. The kaolin was formed by alteration in situ of an alaskite or similar pegmatitic derivative. Extent of alteration varies widely within comparatively short distances; the resultant material ranges from slightly plastic kaolin, containing an excess of free quartz and undecomposed feldspar, to extremely plastic, fine-grained, thoroughly hydrated kaolin. The deposit appears to form an elongated zone that has a general northeast strike (Dietrich, 1928).

The Merrick kaolin deposit is in the N½NW¼NW¼ sec. 36, T. 14 S., R. 1 E., S.B.M., on the west flank of El Cajon Mountain, and appears to be an extension of the El Cajon deposit. At the Merrick deposit, buff, dark-red, and white clay is poorly exposed in a zone that is 20 to 40 ft

wide, 200 ft long, and strikes N. 60° E. Weber (1963) suggested the clay may be a product of hydrothermal alteration along a fault and concluded that the property is of little commercial interest because of its small size and poor accessibility.

With the possible exception of the Daley copper mine, the known mineral deposits on or near the reservation are limited in size and economic potential. However, the local geology does not preclude discovery of other ore bodies similar to that of the Daley deposit. Consequently, a reconnaissance sampling program on the rancheria is justifiable.

CAPITAN GRANDE INDIAN RESERVATION

Location

The Capitan Grande Indian Reservation is one of the largest reservations in Southern California, consisting of 15,753 acres. It is about 38 mi east of San Diego and surrounds a portion of the El Capitan Reservoir, a source of water for the city of San Diego (Figure 23). Tribal headquarters is in Alpine, about 15 mi west of the reservation. No one lives on the reservation and road access is poor.

The reservation occupies a region of strongly dissected mountainous terrain, traversed by a few unimproved roads. Total relief is about 2,000 ft and slopes are locally steep. Climate in the area is generally mild and warm, with rainfall averaging about 15 in. per year.

Geology

The entire Capitan Grande Indian Reservation is underlain by rocks of the Cretaceous age Southern California batholith (Figure 24). In the western part of the reservation (west of 116°45'), these rocks have not been differentiated, but consist primarily of granitic rocks of tonalitic composition (Weber, 1963).

East of 116°45', the batholitic rocks have been subdivided into three units (Everhart, 1951). The predominant rock is a light-gray, medium- to coarse-grained biotite-hornblende tonalite, generally termed the Bonsall tonalite. It is a massive rock which commonly forms large boulders. On close inspection, the rock is generally foliated, with the overall foliation oriented northwest; it generally contains common small pancake-shaped dark inclusions.

Another tonalite, termed the Green Valley tonalite, occurs in the northern part of the reservation. This is a massive to foliated darker gray and finer-grained quartz-diorite than the Bonsall tonalite. The darker color is a result of a greater amount of biotite and hornblende and a lesser amount of quartz. It generally weathers to form smaller boulders than the Bonsall tonalite.

In the southeastern part of the reservation is a small area underlain by gabbro. This gabbro is generally termed the Cuyamaca or San Marcos gabbro. The gabbro is a massive hornblende-rich gabbro which weathers to give rise to a reddish-brown soil studded with small boulders of fresh gabbro.

Mineral Resources

No mineral deposits are reported within the boundaries of the Capitan Grande Indian Reservation. However, in the surrounding area a number of mines and prospects exist in rocks similar to those occurring on the reservation (Weber, 1963, pl. 1). Reported commodities in these mines include gold, uranium, and feldspar.

The Allanite (Keeney) uranium prospect is near the northwest corner of the Capitan Grande Reservation in the NW¼NE¼ sec. 9, T. 14 S., R. 2 E., S.B.M. (Figure 23). The deposit consists of a pegmatite dike, 8 to 10 ft thick and several hundred feet long, that strikes N. 65° and dips 55° N. (Weber, 1963). A border zone, 2 to 3 ft thick, is composed chiefly of graphic granite with sparse blades of biotite, up to 4 in. long, and associated allanite. Allanite is a monoclinic member of the epidote group that commonly contains some thorium and is therefore weakly to moderately radioactive (Thrush, 1968). Mining activity on the property has been minimal, no production has been recorded.

The Spanish Bayonet Mine is about a mile east of the Capitan Grande Reservation, near the center of the W½ sec. 35, T. 14 S., R. 3 E., S.B.M. The property consists of a feldspar deposit mined by open pit in the mid-1940's (Weber, 1963; Everhart, 1951). The deposit consists of a pegmatite dike containing potassic feldspar and pale rose-colored quartz in masses up to 12 in. in maximum dimension. Weber (1963) estimated several hundred tons of material were removed.

Gold deposits in San Diego County commonly occur in Cretaceous granitic rocks, similar to those that underlie the Capitan Grande Indian Reservation (Weber, 1963, pl. 1). Most of these deposits are relatively small and were subeconomic at previous low gold prices. However, the recent dramatic increase in the price of gold may make exploitation of some of the deposits economically feasible.

The lack of reported mineral occurrences on the Capitan Grande Indian Reservation may be due largely to a lack of precious exploration. Considering the large size of the reservation and consequent increased potential for discovery of minerals, a geochemical sampling program is recommended. In particular, sampling of the numerous stream drainages for gold and other metals should be combined with a general reconnaissance of rock outcrops.

VIEJAS INDIAN RANCHERIA

Location

The Viejas Rancheria adjoins State Highway 80 in San Diego County, California, approximately 33 mi east of San Diego (Figure 25). The Indian population in 1971 was 98 persons. The rancheria consists of 1,609 acres comprising the Viejas Valley. Average elevation is about 2,400 ft and maximum relief does not exceed 500 ft. Climate in the valley is temperate with warm summers and mild winters; rainfall averages about 20 in. per year (Merriam, 1951).

Geology

The geology of the Viejas Indian Rancheria consists largely of an alluviated valley, Viejas Valley, bordered by hills underlain by pre-batholithic schist and plutonic rocks of the Cretaceous age Southern California batholith (Figure 26).

The pre-batholithic rock consists primarily of a layered biotite-quartz-feldspar schist with minor local occurrences of metaquartzite and hornblende-bearing schist (Todd, 1978).

The most common rock on the rancheria is the tonalite of Las Bancas. This tonalite has the composition of pyroxene-biotite tonalite and hornblende-biotite tonalite. A small area in the northern part of the reservation is underlain by gabbro, generally termed the Cuyamaca gabbro (Todd, 1978). The gabbro weathers relatively readily giving rise to a reddish-brown soil studded with small boulders of disintegration.

Some of the hillside slopes on the western and eastern ends of the rancheria are mantled with boulderly deposits of colluvium. Viejas Valley is underlain by unconsolidated gray sandy alluvium.

Several small northerly-oriented unnamed faults or inferred faults occur in the western and southeastern parts of the rancheria.

Mineral Resources

The Viejas Rancheria contains no known mineral deposits. Everhart (1951) mapped the geology of the Guyamaca Peak Quadrangle, which includes the rancheria, and examined the economic potential of the area. The Viejas Mountain gold prospect, in sec. 19, T. 15 S., R. 3 E., about ¾ mi west of the rancheria (Figure 25), is described by Everhart as follows:

> It consists of a single tunnel driven 128 feet in weathered norite by the Indians of the Viejas Reservation in 1940 under the auspices of the Civilian Conservation Corps. No sign of a vein or mineralized rock was noted in the tunnel, but one of the miners has reported that "very small amounts" of gold were taken from the workings.

SYCUAN INDIAN RESERVATION

Location

The Sycuan (Sequan) Indian Reservation, comprising all 640 acres of sec. 13, T. 16 S., R. 1 E., S.B.M. (Figure 27), is about 20 mi east of San Diego and 6 mi east of El Cajon. A paved county road passes within ¼ mi of the reservation, providing easy access. In 1971, 31 Indians resided on or adjacent to the reservation.

Climate on the reservation is mild with an average annual rainfall of less than 10 in. (Merriam, 1951). Elevations range from 600 ft, along the banks of the North Fork of the Sweetwater River, to nearly 1,500 ft in the southeast quarter of the reservation.

Geology

The Sycuan Indian Reservation is underlain by plutonic rocks of the Cretaceous age Southern California batholith (Todd, 1980) (Figure 28).

Gabbro, generally termed the Cuyamaca gabbro, is the predominant rock present, occurring in the central and southern part of the reservation. The gabbro is mainly a massive hornblende-rich gabbro, which weathers to a reddish-brown soil studded with small boulders of unweathered gabbro. The northern part of the reservation is underlain by a tonalite, termed the tonalite of Granite Mountain (Todd, 1980).

Mineral Resources

The Sycuan Indian Reservation has no reported mineral deposits, although the area is underlain by granitic rocks of Cretaceous age that contain mineral deposits in other parts of the county. The only mineral occurrences reported near the reservation are a dumortierite exposure about 3 mi northeast and a feldspar mine about 1 mi to the southwest.

The Dehesa dumortierite deposit, in the N½NW¼NE¼ sec. 9, T. 16 S., R. 2 E., S.B.M., one of the first discoveries of dumortierite in the United States, was described in some detail by Schaller (1905). The dumortierite occurs in a crudely tabular body that is composed chiefly of quartz, strikes N. 70° W. and dips 40° to 55° NE. The deposit has not been mined commercially and is presently of interest only to mineral collectors (Weber, 1963). Dumortierite is an aluminum-borosilicate used extensively in the manufacture of spark-plug porcelain and other special refractories.

The McGinty Mountain feldspar deposit, in the NE¼ sec. 27, T. 16 S, R. 1 E., was discovered in 1900 and was worked until about 1930, with an estimated total production of about 7,000 t (Weber,

1963). The final product, referred to as "Cornwall stone," was used in the manufacture of a hard, white, vitrified tile known by the trade name of "Kaospar." The deposit consists of a silicified alaskite dike crosscutting gabbro along a northerly strike. Tucker (1925) reported the composition of the alaskite to be: 77.68 percent silica, 15.97 percent alumina, 2.80 percent lime, 0.13 percent iron, 0.72 percent manganese, and 2.04 percent alkalies.

CAMPO INDIAN RESERVATION

Location

The Campo Indian Reservation is in T. 17 and 18 S., R. 5 and 6 E., San Diego County, California, about 55 mi east of San Diego (Figure 29). The reservation can be reached from San Diego by U.S. Highway 80 or State Highway 94. The San Diego and Arizona Eastern Railroad crosses the southern portion of the reservation. Total area of the reservation is 15,010 acres, with one separate portion of approximately 600 acres situated about 4 mi west. In 1971, 30 Indians lived on the reservation.

Climate in the area is generally mild with hot summers and mild winters; rainfall averages about 20 in. per year (Ellis and Lee, 1919). Elevations on the reservation range between about 2,800 and 4,500 ft.

Geology

The entire Campo Indian Reservation is underlain by tonalite, termed the La Posta quartz diorite (tonalite) (Olmsted, 1953), part of the Cretaceous age southern California batholith (Figure 30). It is a light gray, massive-appearing, sphene-bearing, biotite-hornblende, quartz-diorite (tonalite). It typically weathers to form extensive gray-colored deposits of disintegrated tonalite (gruss). Commonly but less widespread, it weathers to form large fresh boulders of disintegration.

Thin pegmatite and aplite dikes, also part of the batholith, cut the tonalite. These light-colored dikes range from fine- to very coarse-grained and consist principally of quartz and feldspar. Sandy and cobbly gray unconsolidated Holocene alluvium occurs along the bottoms of the larger stream beds.

Mineral Resources

No mineral deposits are reported within the boundaries of the Campo Indian Reservation. The land surface is underlain by large areas of decomposed granitic rocks which are easily mined and are excellent for road surfacing and similar uses. Unfortunately, this material is very abundant in San Diego County at locations much closer to markets. Two quarries in decomposed granite lie just outside the reservation boundary near Cameron Corners (Figure 29). One is located in the NE¼NW¼ sec. 4, T. 18 S., R. 5 E., and is operated by San Diego County for the purpose of road maintenance. The other is an abandoned pit located in the NW¼NW¼ sec. 10, along State Highway 94.

LA POSTA INDIAN RESERVATION

Location

The La Posta Indian Reservation is in eastern San Diego County and adjoins the western edge of the Campo and Manzanita Reservations. A small separate tract of 200 acres is about a mile northwest from the main portion of the reservation (Figure 31). U. S. Highway 80 traverses the southwest corner of the reservation and provides access from San Diego, 50 mi to the west. The reservation has a total area of 3,672 acres and no reported population (U. S. Department of Commerce, 1974).

The climate is relatively mild; average annual rainfall is about 20 in. (Ellis and Lee, 1919). Elevations range between about 3,500 and 4,500 ft.

Geology

The main parcel of the La Posta Indian Reservation is underlain mainly by granitic rocks of the Cretaceous-age Southern California batholith, which here is mainly tonalite, termed the La Posta tonalite (Figure 32). The tonalite is a gray, massive-appearing, sphene-bearing biotite-hornblende tonalite. It typically weathers to form extensive gray-colored deposits of disintegrated tonalite (gruss), that contains fresh boulders of tonalite in some places. Some hybrid metamorphic and granitic rock occur in the northeastern part of the parcel.

The smaller parcel is underlain by a mixture of the tonalite of Las Bancas and the tonalite of Granite Mountain (Todd, 1979). The tonalite of Las Bancas consists of pyroxene-biotite tonalite, hornblende-biotite tonalite, and lesser amounts of quartz gabbro. The tonalite of Granite Mountain is a biotite-hornblende tonalite. Thin gray unconsolidated alluvium underlies some of the northeastern part of the reservation. Four small unnamed northeast-striking faults occur in the smaller reservation parcel.

Mineral Resources

No mineral occurrences are reported on the La Posta Indian Reservation. The Metal Mountain Mining District, 1 to 2 mi north of the reservation (Figure 31), contains deposits of tungsten, feldspar, and gold, and is described in more detail in the section on the Manzanita Indian Reservation. The deposits occur in metamorphic rocks that do not crop out within the boundaries of the La Posta Reservation. Large tonnages of decomposed granite on the reservation are available for local use in road repair and construction.

MANZANITA INDIAN RESERVATION

Location

The Manzanita Indian Reservation is 57 mi east of San Diego, California, and can be reached via U. S. Highway 80, which passes about 2 mi south of its southern boundary. The reservation consists of 3,379 acres in T. 16 S., R. 6 E. (Figure 31). In 1971, only 7 Indians resided on or adjacent to the reservation.

Elevations on the reservation range between 3,600 and about 4,900 ft. The climate is moderate to mild with annual precipitation of about 20 in. Temperatures range from a high of 106° F to a low of 12° F.

Geology

The Manzanita Indian Reservation is underlain mainly by tonalite, termed the La Posta quartz diorite (tonalite) (Olmsted, 1953), part of the Cretaceous-age Southern California batholith. It is a light-gray, massive-appearing, sphene-bearing, biotite-hornblende, quartz-diorite (tonalite). It typically weathers to form extensive gray-colored deposits of disintegrated tonalite (gruss) with large fresh residual boulders of tonalite in places. A narrow strip along the northwestern part of the reservation is underlain by mixed granitic rock and schist.

Pegmatite and aplite dikes, also part of the batholith, cut the tonalite. These light-colored dikes range from fine- to very coarse-grained and consist principally of quartz and feldspar. Sandy and cobbly gray unconsolidated Holocene alluvium occurs along the bottoms of the larger stream beds.

Mineral Resources

No mineral deposits are recorded within the boundaries of the Manzanita Indian Reservation. A number of deposits associated with the Metal Mountain mining district lie within a mile or so of the northwest corner of the reservation (Weber, 1963). However, the host rocks for these deposits do not appear to crop out on the reservation, which is largely underlain by Cretaceous granite.

The mineral occurrence nearest reservation boundaries consists of the Crestline and Gem Spar Claims, in the E½ sec. 21, T. 16 S., R. 6 E. (Figure 31). The property is explored by shallow cuts and trenches across several pegmatite dikes that occur in dark-gray quartz-biotite schist (Weber, 1963). The dikes are 100 to 150 ft long, 3 to 6 ft thick, and are composed chiefly of quartz with a small proportion of large feldspar crystals. The property has had no apparent production.

The Buckthorn Mine is in the SE¼ sec. 16, T. 16 S., R. 6 E., about ½ mi northwest of the northwest corner of the reservation (Figure 31). The mine was worked intermittently between 1926 and 1937 and produced about 2,500 t of feldspar with a smaller tonnage of quartz (Weber, 1963). The deposit consists of three pegmatite dikes in schistose country rock. Workings include an open pit and underground drifts. Weber (1963) reported several thousand tons of quartz and an undetermined tonnage of feldspar remaining beneath the old workings and within extensions of the dikes.

The Metal Mountain tungsten mine is about a mile northwest of the reservation in the S½ sec. 9 and the NW¼ sec. 16, T. 16 S., R. 6 E. The Blackstone, Last Dollar, Winatoma, and Morning Glory Prospects are similar occurrences that lie within a mile of the reservation (Figure 31). The Metal Mountain district was first prospected in the 1890's for lead and silver and it was not until the 1950's that tungsten was discovered. The tungsten occurs in quartz veins as scheelite, locally altered to tungstite, along with minor amounts of ferberite. Pyrite, silver-bearing galena, sphalerite, cerussite, and gold are also present in the veins. The deposits at the Metal Mountain Mine have been developed by shafts, adits, and trenches.

CUYAPAIPE INDIAN RESERVATION

Location

The Cuyapaipe Indian Reservation, consisting of 4,100 acres in T. 15 S., R. 6 E. (Figure 33), is situated in eastern San Diego County, California, about 75 mi east of San Diego. Elevations range between 3,200 ft and 6,400 ft, and the climate is generally mild with an average annual rainfall of over 20 in. In 1969, no Indians resided on the reservation.

Geology

The Cuyapaipe Indian Reservation is underlain by rocks of the Cretaceous age Southern California batholith, some prebatholithic schist, and mixed prebatholithic gneiss and granitic rocks (Figure 34). That part of the reservation east of 116°22.5' is underlain by undifferentiated granitic rock with a mixture of this rock and prebatholithic biotite-bearing schist and gneiss along the eastern edge of the reservation (Weber, 1963). A small amount of schist, relatively free of granitic material, occurs in the southeastern part of the reservation.

The part of the reservation west of 116°22.5' is underlain primarily by tonalite of Las Bancas (Todd, 1978). This tonalite is principally a gray, medium-grained, pyroxene-biotite tonalite and hornblende-biotite tonalite. Along its northwestern extent, it is a leucocratic tonalite and granodiorite.

The northwestern part of the reservation is underlain by prebatholithic schist. Here the schist consists of layered biotite-bearing quartzo-feldspathic schist and micaceous feldspathic schist, and locally hornblende-bearing schist. Thin deposits of gray unconsolidated alluvium occur along Thing Valley.

Several small unnamed faults occur in the northwestern part of the reservation.

Mineral Resources

No mineral occurrences are reported on the Cuyapaipe Reservation. Deposits of tungsten, gold, and feldspar are found about 2 mi south of the reservation in the Metal Mountain mining district (see discussion in section on Manzanita Indian Reservation). Host rocks for these deposits extend into the southeast corner of the reservation and similar rocks also crop out in the northwest corner. A field reconnaissance of these rock outcrops is recommended to determine if similar mineral deposits are present.

LOS COYOTES INDIAN RESERVATION

Location

The Los Coyotes Indian Reservation consists of 25,050 acres in T. 10 and 11 S., R. 4 and 5 E., San Diego County, California (Figure 35). The terrain is mostly mountainous, with elevations ranging between 6,533 ft on Hot Springs Mountain to 3,440 ft near the southwest corner of the reservation.

The nearest sizable town is Ramona, which lies 31 mi to the southwest via State Highways 78 and 72. State Highway 79 passes through Warner Springs, which is about 1 mi west of the reservation. Weather is moderate with rainfall averaging around 18 in. per year (Ellis and Lee, 1919). In 1971, 42 Indians resided on or adjacent to the reservation.

Geology

The Los Coyotes Indian Reservation is underlain by granitic rock of the Cretaceous-age Southern California, prebatholithic schist and gneiss, and mixtures of the two (Figure 36). The granitic rocks underlying most of the reservation are primarily a medium- to coarse-grained biotite-hornblende tonalite and lesser amounts of biotite-granodiorite (Weber, 1963). These rocks are light-gray, massive, and commonly weather to form large boulders.

Prebatholithic schist occurs in the southeastern part of the reservation. The schist consists of layered biotite-bearing quartzofeldspathic schist and lesser amounts of hornblende-bearing schist. In the northwestern part of the reservation, the rocks consist of a mixture of the granitic rocks and schist and gneiss.

Several small unnamed northwest-striking faults are located in the northeastern part of the reservation.

Mineral Resources

The Los Coyotes Indian Reservation is underlain by a series of granitic and metasedimentary rocks of Cretaceous age, which in other parts of San Diego County contain deposits of gold, tungsten, gem minerals, and feldspar. The Los Coyotes tungsten prospect is the only mineral deposit reported within the boundaries of the reservation. It is near the east edge of the SE¼SE¼ sec. 24, T. 10 S., R. 4 E., S.B.M., about 6¾ mi east of Warner Springs (Figure 35). Workings consist of a shallow cut across a zone of scheelite-bearing tactite that is several hundred feet long and from 5 to 10 ft wide where exposed. The zone strikes northward and dips steeply east near the contact between granitic and metasedimentary rocks (Weber, 1963).

The Montezuma mining district, about ½ mi south of the reservation in secs. 10 and 11, T. 11 S., R. 4 E., S.B.M., contains commercial-grade deposits of limestone and gold. The limestone deposits occur in Cretaceous metasedimentary rocks that extend in a belt, several miles wide, across the southeast corner of the reservation. The principal producer, the Verruga marble deposit, was worked from 1921 to 1923 by the Verruga Marble Company of San Diego for building stone (Figure 35). The quarried stone was cut and polished on the property and used in the construction of several buildings in San Diego. Recently (1956), an adjoining property, the White Peak Claim, was worked for the production of roofing granules and chicken grit (Stewart, 1958).

The principal gold deposit in the Montezuma district is the Montezuma Mine, in sec. 10, T. 13 S., R. 4 E., S.B.M. (Figure 35). This property was first prospected in the 1890's, but apparently the principal work was carried out in about 1910 when the property was developed by a 230-ft shaft with about 2,000 ft of appended level workings (Weber,

1963). The gold occurs in a quartz vein that is about 4 ft wide, strikes N. 65° E. and dips 70° NW. Production values are not known and the workings are presently inaccessible.

The Payoff tungsten mine is in the N½N½ sec. 6, T. 11 S., R. 5 E., S.B.M., about ¼ mi south of the southeast corner of the Los Coyotes Reservation (Figure 35). This deposit was discovered in 1955 and was worked in 1955 and 1956. A narrow, northeast-trending vertical zone of scheelite-bearing tactite is interlayered with rocks that consist chiefly of biotite-quartz-sericite schist (Weber, 1963). Production exceeded 150 t of ore averaging 1 percent tungsten oxide (WO_3). Workings include a 300-ft adit and two winzes, with sub-levels off the winzes.

Near the northeast corner of the reservation in the NW¼ sec. 5, T. 10 S., R. 5 E., S.B.M., an occurrence of tin is reported at the Katherine Prospect (Weber, 1963). Small pendants of slate and mica schist in granitic rocks contain very small amounts of tin, although no megascopic tin minerals are present (W. T. Bean, U.S. Bureau of Mines, unpub. report, 1949). Two small prospects, one for tourmaline and the other for tungsten, are in sec. 14, T. 10 S., R. 3 E., about 2 mi west of the reservation. No production is reported from any of these prospects.

Warner Hot Springs is about 1 mi west of the western boundary of the reservation (Figure 35). In the early part of the century, Warner Springs consisted of six or more vents that discharged about 150 gal of water a minute at a maximum observed temperature of 159° F (Waring, 1915). The springs, which have been developed into a well-known resort, appear to be associated with the northwest-southeast-trending Agua Caliente fault zone that passes just to the west of the reservation. Numerous springs also occur on the reservation, especially in the area around Hot Springs Mountain (Figure 35). No information is available on water temperatures.

The Los Coyotes Reservation would appear to warrant a geologic reconnaissance, including a program of geochemical sampling, to determine the presence of any economic mineral deposits. The program should include an assessment of geothermal potential and a reevaluation of the Los Coyotes tungsten prospect, in light of recent price increases for tungsten.

CAHUILLA INDIAN RESERVATION

Location

The Cahuilla Indian Reservation consists of 18,272 acres in T. 7 and 8 S., R. 2 and 3 E., S.B.M., Riverside County, California (Figure 37). The reservation has a population of about 23 Indians. Highway 71 traverses the reservation and provides a link with tribal headquarters in Hemet, California, 20 mi to the northwest.

The reservation largely occupies Cahuilla and Terwilliger Valleys and associated alluvial fans. Relief is generally low, with elevations between 3,400 and 4,500 ft; the climate is warm and sunny throughout most of the year. Access is very good throughout the reservation.

Geology

The Cahuilla Indian Reservation is underlain by granitic rock of the Southern California batholith of Cretaceous age, which is in part overlain by the Bautista beds and alluvial-valley fill (Sharp, 1967) (Figure 38). On the reservation, this granitic rock is a homogeneous biotite-hornblende tonalite, generally weathering to form large boulders.

The Bautista beds of Pleistocene age, cropping out in the Terwilliger Valley area, rest unconformably upon the tonalite. These beds, once continuous across the valley, have been dissected, giving rise to slightly elevated flattish-topped hills. The beds consist of grayish thick-bedded, coarse-grained, crudely bedded, and poorly indurated sediments. The valley areas are underlain by grayish Holocene alluvium resting on either the tonalite or Bautista beds.

Mineral Resources

The mineral potential of the Cahuilla Reservation appears to be low. Mesozoic granitic rocks of the Southern California batholith appear to underlie large portions of the reservation (Larsen, 1948). These rocks host pegmatite veins that have been mined for feldspar and silica in surrounding areas, notably at the Williamson Mine to the northwest of the reservation (Figure 37) and the Lang deposit, about 2 mi to the southwest (Tucker and Sampson, 1929). No such mineral occurrences have been reported on the reservation.

Kunz (1905) reported considerable mining activity during the early part of this century in the region around Cahuilla Mountain, about 3 mi northwest of the reservation. Several pegmatites produced gem-quality crystals of tourmaline, kunzite, and beryl. It is not clear from the report if the pegmatite zones extend onto the Cahuilla Reservation. A search of the reservation for such an extension of the gem-bearing zones may be warranted.

Cahuilla and Terwilliger Valleys are underlain largely by alluvial deposits (Moyle, 1976; Rogers, 1965). The associated sand and gravel deposits are adequate for local use, but the lack of nearby markets probably precludes their development as an economic commodity.

SANTA ROSA INDIAN RESERVATION

Location

The Santa Rosa Indian Reservation is in Riverside County, California, approximately 13 mi south of Palm Springs, in T. 7 S., and R. 4 and 5 E., S.B.M. Tribal headquarters is in Hemet, California, 38 mi to the northwest via Highway 74, which crosses a portion of the reservation (Figure 39). The reservation is made up of four separate parcels of land with a total area of about 11,093 acres and a population of about 7 Indians.

The largest parcel of land is centered on a relatively low-lying area of desert terrain with elevations ranging from about 4,000 to 5,800 ft. The remaining portions of the reservation are situated in the Santa Rosa Mountains, with elevations reaching 8,716 ft. The climate is arid with an average rainfall of about 7 in. per year and temperature extremes of 109° F and 16° F. Road access is generally poor throughout most of the reservation.

Geology

The largest parcel of the Santa Rosa Indian Reservation is underlain by pre-Cretaceous metamorphic rocks and granitic rocks of the Cretaceous age Southern California batholith (Sharp, 1967) (Figure 40). Overlying these basement rocks are extensive deposits of the Bautista beds and younger alluvium.

The metamorphic rock consists of layered biotite schist and gneiss. The layering is produced by alternating biotite-rich and biotite-poor layers. Discontinuous layers of marble and associated skarn occur locally.

In the southwestern part of sec. 27, T. 7 S., R. 4 E., S.B.M., several small patches of metamorphic rocks have been thrust over the Bautista beds.

Granitic rocks of the Southern California batholith intrude the metamorphic rock. Massive to foliated hornblende-biotite tonalite is the most widespread granitic rock. In the western part, sec. 3, is an occurrence of a medium- to coarse-grained quartz monzonite which generally contains some garnets. In the northwestern part of sec. 22, the granitic rock is a foliated biotite-quartz monzonite. Unconformably overlying the basement rocks are extensive occurrences of the Bautista beds of Pleistocene age. These beds consist of grayish, thick-bedded, coarse-grained to conglomeratic, crudely bedded, and poorly indurated sediments.

Flat-lying terrace sands and gravels of late Pleistocene age overlie basement rocks and the Bautista beds in the southwestern part of the

reservation, and unconsolidated Holocene alluvium occurs along the floor of Vandeventer Flat.

The southwestern part of the reservation is crossed by the seismically active Buck Ridge fault, a major fault which is part of the San Jacinto fault complex.

The part of the reservation consisting of sec. 32, T. 7 S., R. 5 E., S.B.M., is underlain by metamorphic rock, granitic rock (biotite-hornblende tonalite), and Bautista beds similar to those described for The larger reservation parcel. An occurrence of skarn (tactite) occurs in the southeastern part of sec. 32.

The part of the reservation consisting of sec. 34, T. 7 5, R. 5 E., S.B.M., is underlain by granitic rock (biotite-hornblende tonalite of the Cretaceous-age Southern California batholith), except for the northeastern most corner, where there is a small amount of prebatholithic schist and gneiss. The part of the reservation consisting of sec. 36 is underlain by the same biotite-hornblende tonalite with septa of gneiss and schist in the southwest and northeast parts of the section.

Mineral Resources

No mineral deposits or mining activities have been reported within the boundaries of the reservation. However, numerous mines within 2 or 3 mi of the reservation have produced small-to-moderate quantities of gold, tungsten, beryllium, asbestos, and limestone (Table 1). The more prominent of these mines are shown in Figure 39. The mineral deposits are associated with Mesozoic granitic and metamorphic rocks, which extend onto the northern and eastern portions of the reservation (Rogers,

1965). For this reason, similar economic deposits may occur on reservation land, and a reconnaissance and geochemical sampling program is recommended.

RAMONA INDIAN RESERVATION

Location

The Ramona Indian Reservation is in the western foothills of the San Jacinto Mountains, on the western slope of Thomas Mountain, in T. 6 and 7 S., R. 3 E., S.B.M. (Figure 41). The reservation is unpopulated and has an area of 560 acres. Access is by unimproved road from Highway 71. The terrain is mountainous and the climate is hot and dry.

Geology

The Ramona Indian Reservation is in a topographically low area along the San Jacinto fault zone which here consists of several individual faults (Sharp, 1967) (Figure 42). Basement rocks consist of a minor occurrence of pre-Cretaceous biotite gneiss in SW¼ sec. 30, T. 6 S., R. 3 W., S.B.M. The westernmost part of a tonalite body extends into the eastern part of the reservation. This tonalite, part of the Cretaceous-age Southern California batholith, is a massive, coarse-grained, sphene-rich, hornblende-biotite tonalite. In the western part of the reservation, Bautista beds of Pleistocene age occur. They consist of a sequence of thick-bedded gray coarse-grained, sandy to conglomeratic, and mainly nonindurated poorly bedded sediments. The bedding in the Bautista beds is variable, but overall, dips at moderate to steep angles to the northeast. Unconformably overlying the Bautista beds are unconsolidated, poorly bedded deposits of terrace sands and gravels of late Pleistocene age.

Along the valley floor are deposits of unconsolidated Quaternary coarse-grained alluvium.

The San Jacinto fault, extending the length of the reservation, is one of the most seismically active faults in California.

Mineral Resources

The Ramona Reservation falls within a region of gemstone occurrences informally known as the Thomas Mountain and Coahuila Mountain districts (Jahns and Wright, 1951). The first discovery of gem tourmalines in California was made in 1872 on the south slope of Thomas Mountain in sec. 28, T. 6 S., R. 3 E., (Figure 41). Several mines in the area were worked around the turn of the century and produced gem-quality tourmaline, quartz, beryl, and kunzite. The mines on Thomas Mountain are in pegmatite dikes that are as much as 50 ft wide and contain multicolored tourmaline crystals as large as 4 in. across (Kunz, 1905).

The Columbia, San Jacinto, and California Mines on Thomas Mountain are three of the oldest gem mines in the State, and have produced many beautiful gems in the past (Kunz, 1905; Murdoch and Webb, 1956). The California Mine yielded $10,000 worth of green, pink, red, and black tourmaline and rose quartz in 1894 (Merrill, 1917). The Fano (Simmons) Mine, about 4 mi west of the reservation in the NW¼SW¼ sec. 33, T. 6 S., R. 2 E., was discovered in 1902, and by 1905 had produced 26 lb of kunzite, 250 lb of beryl, 200 lb of quartz crystal, 1 t of lepidolite, and about 40 lb of amblygonite (Kunz, 1905; Merrill, 1917; Murdoch and Webb, 1956).

Although none of the reported mines fall within the boundaries of the reservation, the degree of early mining activity in the surrounding area justifies a reconnaissance field study of the reservation. This is particularly true in light of the recent dramatic rise in the prices of semiprecious gems and mineral specimens.

SOBOBA INDIAN RESERVATION

Location

The Soboba Indian Reservation is in T. 4 and 5 S., R. 1 E., S.B.M., Riverside County, California. The reservation covers an area of 5,036 acres and has a population of about 178 Indians. Tribal headquarters is in San Jacinto and travel facilities are available in Hemet, 4 mi southwest.

The reservation lies in the foothills of the San Jacinto Mountains and occupies the Poppet and Indian Creek drainage basins, as well as a portion of the San Jacinto River Valley (Figure 43). Total relief is about 800 ft and road access is good. The climate is mild; rainfall averages 4.7 in. per year.

Geology

The northwestern most part of the Soboba Indian Reservation, SE¼, sec. 20, T. 4 S., R. 1 E., S.B.M., is underlain by metasedimentary rocks of pre-middle Cretaceous age (Figure 44). This rock in most places is underlain by Quaternary nonmarine sediments with alluvium occurring along canyon floors and in the San Jacinto Valley (Fraser, 1931). The Quaternary deposits, known as the Bautista beds, consist of mainly gray, thick and poorly bedded, coarse-grained, sandy to locally conglomeratic sandstone with local thin greenish-gray silty beds, some of which contain fossil plant remains. Most of the sediments are composed of granitic detritus derived from the granitic rocks underlying the San Jacinto Mountains east of the reservation. Landslides are common in these sediments. Extensive occurrence of coarse sandy alluvium occurs along the floor of Poppet Creek, Indian Creek, and the San Jacinto Valley.

The northern part of the reservation is crossed by the Hot Springs fault, an east-striking fault intersecting the San Jacinto (Claremont) fault 1 mi west of the reservation. The northwest-striking San Jacinto (Claremont) fault occurs along the northern edge of the San Jacinto Valley at the western part of the reservation. The San Jacinto fault is one of the most seismically active faults in California.

Mineral Resources

No mines or mineral occurrences are known on the reservation and the mineral potential appears low. Sand and gravel deposits occur on the reservation in Poppet Creek Canyon and in the floodplain of the San Jacinto River. If nearby markets are available, exploitation of these deposits may be economically feasible. A cryptic reference to the Juaro Canyon Stone Quarry, at the northern edge of the reservation in SW¼ sec. 20, T. 4 S., R. 1 E., provides no information on rock type, uses, or production (California Division of Mines, 1968, unpublished report on Riverside County).

Soboba Hot Springs are 1 mi northwest of the reservation in NW¼NW¼ sec. 30, T. 4 S., R. 1 E., (Figure 43). Deeply circulating groundwater, with a temperature range of 70° to 118° F., flows from springs in the Claremont-San Jacinto fault zone (Tucker and Sampson, 1945; Waring, 1965). Because this fault zone crosses the southwestern part of the reservation, a geothermal potential may exist (Lofgren, 1976). Additional geologic evaluation is needed to assess this potential.

AGUA CALIENTE INDIAN RESERVATION

Location

The Agua Caliente Indian Reservation is in Riverside County, California, generally on even-numbered sections within T. 4 and 5 S., R. 4 and 5 E., S.B.M. (Figure 45). Tribal headquarters is in Palm Springs, parts of which are on reservation land. Total area of the reservation is approximately 25,899 acres and the population consists of about 74 Indians.

Roughly half of the reservation lies in the rugged San Jacinto Mountains, where elevations reach nearly 6,000 ft; the other half falls within the Coachella Valley with elevations as low as approximately 250 ft. The climate is arid and hot; temperatures reach 122° F. during the summer months. Access to the western, mountainous portion of the reservation is poor.

Geology

Those parts of the Agua Caliente Indian Reservation located in the San Jacinto Mountains are underlain by granitic rocks of the Southern California batholith and prebatholithic metamorphic rocks which, in large part, are of sedimentary origin (Dibblee, unpublished U.S. Geological Survey mapping, 1971) (Figure 46). The high eastern parts of the reservation are underlain primarily by schist and gneiss, intruded by masses of granitic rock. Most of the schist and gneiss is well-layered and strikes in a north to northwest direction. Layering is produced primarily by variation in quartz content. Locally, these are pods or lens-shaped masses of marble. In the northwestern parts of the reservation, the marble is more extensive and forms discontinuous lenses and continuous layers ½ mi or greater in length. Most of the marble is coarse grained and off-white in color. A mixture of siliceous minerals in varying quantities is common within the marble. In some places where the marble is in contact with granitic rock, there are local occurrences of skarn (calc-silicate rock). Within the eastern part of the metamorphic rocks, cataclastic-textured schist and gneiss become common. These cataclastically deformed rocks are generally better layered than non-cataclastically deformed schist. Within the cataclastically deformed rocks, quartz and feldspar generally have a ground-out appearance and mafic minerals (for example, biotite) are commonly streaked out.

Intensely cataclastic deformed schist and intermingled granitic rock form a very regular thick unit extending from the northeastern San Jacinto Mountains south along the west side of

Palm Springs and into Palm Canyon. The cataclastic layering in these rocks is pronounced and regular in orientation. The foliation strikes northward and dips moderately to the east. This unit forms the "flatiron" ridges along the east side of the San Jacinto Mountains.

Intruding the metamorphic rocks are numerous bodies of granitic rock, part of the Cretaceous-age Southern California batholith. Granodioritic-composition rock prevails, with more local occurrences of tonalite and diorite. The granodiorite is a coarse-grained relatively light-colored rock bearing biotite or biotite and hornblende, generally weathering to form large boulders. The eastern part of the granodiorite west of Palm Canyon is generally well foliated, reflecting the cataclastic deformation. Here it weathers to form more sheet-like outcrops.

Tonalite and diorite occur less commonly than granodiorite and are most common in the vicinity of Chino Canyon in the northwestern part of the reservation. It is darker gray than the granodiorite and contains abundant hornblende and biotite.

The cataclastic unit along the east side of the San Jacinto Mountains includes a large amount of cataclastically deformed granitic rock intermingled with similarly deformed schist and gneiss.

The valley parts of the reservation are underlain by unconsolidated alluvial units ranging from boulder alluvial fans along the eastern side of the San Jacinto Mountains to extensive dune-sand deposits along the central part of the Coachella Valley.

Active, bouldery alluvial fans extend out from the mouths of canyons along the east side of the mountain. Most impressive are those steep fans such as at the mouth of Chino Canyon. The boulder size decreases down the fan away from the mountains. Many of the fans are subject to active stream wash during times of excessively heavy rainfall.

Away from the mountains, the northern part of the Coachella Valley is covered by cobbly to sandy unconsolidated grayish alluvium with some older deformed, partly indurated alluvium occurring east of U.S. 60 (Edom Hill area). Discontinuous areas of active dune sand are common. Southward in the valley, the grain size of the alluvium decreases and dune sand becomes prevalent in the southeastern part of the reservation.

Mineral Resources

Economic deposits reported to occur on or near the reservation include tungsten, corundum, limestone, and sand and gravel. U.S. Bureau of Mines files indicate the occurrence of corundum on the reservation in sec. 14, T. 5 S., R. 4 E., but provide no additional information on the nature of the deposit.

The Phoenix tungsten deposit is located adjacent to reservation land in sec. 9, T. 5 S., R. 4 E., and consists of scheelite mineralization in sporadic outcrops of calc-silicate rocks along a contact between granite and limestone (Figure 45). Orebodies as much as 18 ft wide are exposed for a distance of 900 ft along a ridge between Andreas and Murray Canyons. The site has several open cuts and a 20 t mill (Tucker and Sampson, 1945).

Potentially economic outcrops of limestone occur on and adjacent to the reservation in secs. 5 and 6, T. 4 S., R. 4 E. in the mountains north of

Chino Canyon and in secs. 25 and 36, T. 5 S., R. 4 E. in Palm Canyon (California Division of Mines, unpublished report on Riverside County; Tucker and Sampson, 1945). No mining activity has been reported in conjunction with these deposits.

Sand and gravel deposits in the Coachella Valley constitute a potentially valuable resource because of the large construction industry in the Palm Springs area. At least one sand and gravel pit is located on the reservation in SE¼NW¼NE¼ sec. 32, T. 4 S., R. 5 E., and several others occur on adjacent lands.

Agua Caliente Hot Springs are on reservation land in SW¼SW¼NW¼ sec. 14, T. 4 S., R. 4 E., at the intersection of Indian Avenue and McCallum Way in Palm Springs (Figure 45). Deeply circulating groundwater with a temperature of 100° F. flows from fractured granite in the Palm Canyon fault zone (Tucker and Sampson, 1945; Waring, 1965). The genetic relationship between the Coachella Valley and the San Andreas fault system suggests the likelihood of other hot springs and high temperature wells on the reservation. The geothermal potential of the reservation is unknown but may be significant.

Recommendations for Further Work

The Agua Caliente Reservation is dispersed over a large area containing many different types of geologic formations, including Mesozoic granitic and metamorphic rocks and Pleistocene to Holocene sedimentary units. The variety of rock types, as well as known mineral deposits of tungsten, corundum, and limestone, suggests a favorable area for a reconnaissance field study. The

study should include an assessment of the economic potential and marketability of limestone and sand and gravel deposits, as well as an evaluation of geothermal potential. A geochemical sampling program should be carried out to determine if gold-bearing units that occur to the south extend onto the reservation.

TORRES MARTINEZ AND CABAZON RESERVATIONS AND AUGUSTINE INDIAN RANCHERIA

Location

The Augustine, Cabazon, and Torres Martinez Reservations are all within the Coachella Valley in the southeastern part of California. The Coachella Valley is part of a broad structural depression, sometimes referred to as the Salton Sea Trough, which constitutes a landward extension of the Gulf of California. The valley floor is relatively flat and predominantly below sea level. The reservations are composed of whole or partial sections of surveyed land that create a checkerboard pattern across the valley floor at the north end of the Salton Sea (Figure 47).

The Augustine Rancheria consists of about 502 uninhabited acres in sec. 18, T. 6 S., R. 8 E. The Cabazon Reservation has a total area of 1,706 acres making up all or part of secs. 19, 30, and 32, T. 5 S., R. 8 E., and sec. 6, T. 7 S., R. 9 E. In 1971, six Indians lived on or adjacent to the Cabazon Reservation. The Torres Martinez Reservation includes approximately 30,329 acres, with a resident population of about 42 Indians. About 9,000 acres of tribal land are submerged beneath the Salton Sea (Figure 47).

The climate in the Coachella Valley is hot and arid. Temperatures range between a high of about 120° F. in July and a low of about 28° F. in mid-winter. Average rainfall is 3.4 in. The valley is crossed by U.S. Highway 60 and State Highways 86 and 111, as well as numerous secondary access roads. Transportation facilities are available in Indio, about a mile northwest of the Cabazon Reservation (Figure 47).

Geology

The Cabezon Indian Reservation and Augustine Rancheria are underlain by unconsolidated alluvial deposits and late Quaternary lake deposits (Rogers, 1965) (Figure 48). The alluvial deposits are unconsolidated gray sand; the lake deposits are generally finer-grained sand and silt. The lake deposits were formed when a prehistoric lake filled a much larger part of the Coachella Valley-Imperial Valley area than the present day Salton Sea.

The Torres Martinez Indian Reservation is located principally within the Coachella Valley-Salton Sea, but the southwestern parts extend onto the eastern part of the Santa Rosa Mountains (Rogers, 1965) (Figure 49 and Figure 50). That part of the reservation in the mountains is underlain by a mixed assemblage of schist and marble intruded by granitic rock of the Southern California batholith. The pre-Cretaceous schist is a relatively well layered biotite schist with layers of variable biotite content and local masses of quartz-rich rock. Discontinuous masses of off-white marble

occur within the schist. Within the marble, included siliceous rock and schist are common. Granitic rock of the Cretaceous-age Southern California batholith intrude the schist and marble.

Locally resting on the metamorphic and granitic rocks that crop out near Wonderstone Wash are Pliocene nonmarine sediments and silicic volcanic rock. The volcanic rock is mainly light-colored rhyolite. The sediments are coarse, moderately well to well-indurated conglomerate. A small area is underlain by finer-grained marine sediments west of Travertine Rock. Pleistocene (?) age conglomeratic sediments occur in the southernmost part and the northeastern part of the reservation. Those in the northeastern part of the reservation (near Box Canyon Wash) are cobbly deposits deformed and cut by the San Andreas fault zone.

Those parts of the reservation located in the Coachella Valley are underlain by unconsolidated alluvial deposits and late Quaternary lake deposits; those parts within the Salton Sea are covered by water. Along the margins of the valley, the alluvium is unconsolidated gray, sandy to cobbly alluvium, which becomes progressively finer-grained towards the flat floor of the valley. The lower parts of the valley are underlain by fine-sandy alluvium and lake beds similar to those in the Cabezon Indian Reservation and Augustine Indian Rancheria. In the vicinity of Travertine Rock are accumulations of unconsolidated dune sand. Much of the eastern part of the reservation is covered by the Salton Sea.

The seismically active San Andreas fault zone forms the eastern margin of the Coachella Valley-Salton trough. This major fault zone crosses diagonally with a northwest orientation on the northeastern part of the reservation (sec. 2 and 12, T. 6 S., R. 9 E., S.B.M.).

Mineral Resources

No producing mines or metallic mineral deposits are reported on any of the Indian lands in the Coachella Valley. Potential mineral resources appear to be limited to industrial rocks and minerals, such as limestone, calcite, sand and gravel, and evaporites, and to metals and nonmetals recovered from the Salton Sea brines. In addition, a significant potential exists for the development of geothermal energy resources and possibly carbon dioxide gas in the Salton Sea region.

Industrial Rocks and Minerals

Limestone deposits crop out in sec. 5, 6, 7, 8, 17, 18, T. 9 S., R. 9 E. (Figure 47). The crystalline limestone or marble is white to buff and is exposed in narrow beds as much as 4,000 ft long and 100 ft thick (Morton, 1977). In the SE¼ of sec. 7, an estimated 750,000 t of marble, containing inclusions of gneiss and schist, are available for quarrying. Chemical analyses of samples from this deposit show the following ranges of composition: 84-96 percent $CaCO_3$, 1.4-4.7 percent $MgCO_3$, 0.23-5.8 percent SiO_2, 0.01-0.61 percent Fe_2O_3, and 0.22-5.7 percent Al_2O_3 (Oesterling and Spurck, 1964).

The Hilton Calcite Deposit is in the S½ sec. 14 and the S½ of sec. 15, T. 10 S., R. 8 E. At least 6,800 lb of sub-optical-grade calcite were produced in the early 1940's and indicated reserves were estimated in 1944 to be about 3,000 t of usable

calcite (Weber, 1963). The calcite occurs with gypsum along joints in the Canebrake conglomerate. This unit strikes northeast and may extend onto tribal lands.

Sand and gravel deposits are present in stream channels, alluvial fans, and shoreline benches of prehistoric Lake Cahuilla (California Division of Mines, 1968, unpublished report on Riverside County) The shoreline deposits may represent important sources of low-cost, commercial concrete aggregate (Morton, 1977). A few permanent sand and gravel quarries are on reservation land (Figure 47), but much road-base material, fill, and riprap are obtained from local sites as a one-time operation.

Pliocene evaporite deposits in the Borrego Formation have been mined for sodium sulfate at the Bertram Mine, in the NE¼ sec. 19, T. 9 S., R. 12 E. (Morton, 1977). The evaporite beds at the mine strike about N. 60° W. and may extend below the Quaternary lake-bed deposits that cover the major portion of the Coachella Valley (Rogers, 19650. It is unknown whether or not the more recent lake-bed units also contain similar evaporite deposits.

Salton Sea Brines

The Salton Sea was formed during 1905 and 1906 by flooding from the Colorado River and the subsequent dissolution of salts from playa deposits in the Coachella Valley. The salinity of the later reached a nearly uniform value of approximately 3,650 ppm in 1907 (VerPlanck, 1958). Subsequent evaporation, and possibly input from subsurface magmatic sources, raised the concentration of salts to about 37,500 ppm by 1970. The composition of the resulting brine is higher in sulfate, carbonate, and calcium, and is slightly lower in chloride and magnesium than normal ocean water (Morton, 1977). Limited production of salt by evaporation of the brine was carried out during the early part of this century (Verplanck, 1958).

Recent research into the extraction of minerals from geothermal brines suggests that both metals and nonmetals can be recovered economically in conjunction with the production of geothermal energy (Blake, 1974). The geothermal brines at the southern end of the Salton Sea contain up to 3,200 ppm iron, 2,000 ppm manganese, 970 ppm zinc, 520 ppm boron, 300 ppm lithium, 141 ppm lead, 10 ppm copper, and 1 ppm silver (Hornburg, 1977). Concentrations of sodium, potassium, and calcium are orders of magnitude higher. The brines are reported to also contain 2 ppm gold and to be capable of nearly doubling the world's present annual production if the Salton Sea geothermal field were fully developed (Mining Engineering, 1979).

Geothermal Energy

A geothermal field, estimated to underlie about 100,000 acres, is centered at the southeast end of the Salton Sea (Berman, 1975). Current interest in exploitation of the field began in 1957, when an exploratory oil well encountered hot brine at depths near 5,000 ft. Recent investigations have concentrated on the area between the southern edge of the Salton Sea and the Mexican border, referred to as the Imperial Valley (Swanberg, 1976). This area has been estimated to have an electrical potential as high as 30,000 MW (Berman, 1975).

It is unclear whether the Imperial Valley geothermal field extends to the northern edge of the Salton Sea or if a similar, deeper, heat source may be present there. A well drilled in sec. 16, T. 6 S., R. 10 E. reportedly produced hot water at an unknown depth (Oesterling and Spurck, 1964). This reported occurrence would seem to warrant further investigation of the Coachella Valley as a possible geothermal resource.

Carbon Dioxide

The production of carbon dioxide, used primarily for the production of dry ice, has been associated with early development efforts in the Imperial Valley geothermal field (Berman, 1975). It appears that the gas is produced through decarbonation of sediments by hot saline solutions generated at depth (Robinson and others, 1976), and migrates along fractures in the overlying sediments, becoming trapped beneath impermeable layers (Morton, 1977). If similar geologic conditions exist beneath the Coachella Valley, a potential for carbon dioxide production may exist.

MORONGO INDIAN RESERVATION

Location

The Morongo Indian Reservation, situated in T. 2 and 3 S., R. 1 and 2 E., S.B.M., Riverside County, California (Figure 51), extends across San Gorgonio Pass into the San Bernardino Mountains to the north and the San Jacinto Mountains to the south. Elevations range between 2,000 and about 5,000 ft. The reservation has an area of 32,252 acres and a population of about 242 Indians. Tribal headquarters is in Banning, at the southwest edge of the reservation. U. S. Highway 99 and State Highway 74 cross the reservation.

Geology

The geology of the Morongo Indian Reservation is extremely varied and complex. Those parts of the reservation north of San Gorgonio Pass are within the San Bernardino Mountains, part of the eastern Transverse Ranges geologic province. Those parts south of the pass are in the San Jacinto Mountains which are located in the northernmost part of the Peninsular Ranges geologic province. The geologic boundary between the two provinces is one of the most fundamental and complicated in California. The geology of the reservation is discussed in two parts--that north of the pass, and that to the south.

North of the pass, most of the reservation is underlain by an undifferentiated complex assemblage of metamorphic rock and lesser amounts of plutonic rock (Allen, 1957) (Figure 52). This assemblage is composed primarily of a gray gneiss with lesser amounts of schist and intermediate composition plutonic rocks, most of which have been sheared and commonly cataclastically deformed and cut by granitic pegmatite dikes. Most of the gneiss and schist is not well layered, but is relatively well foliated; biotite-hornblende-feldspar-quartz gneiss is the most common rock type. Masses of discontinuous lensoidal layered gneiss are common. The orientation of the layering

is varied, but northwest strikes predominate in the eastern part of this unit. Locally, white mica-bearing gneiss occurs. West of the lower part of Stubbe Canyon the manganese-bearing epidote mineral piedmontite occurs, imparting a reddish color to the gneiss.

The age of the gneiss is unknown other than it is pre-middle Cretaceous and may be as old as Precambrian. The deformed plutonic rocks, considered to be of Cretaceous age, are mainly of tonalitic or granodioritic composition, gray in color, medium-grained, generally possess a foliation, and contain biotite and hornblende as mafic minerals.

Cutting this assemblage of gneiss and plutonic rock are thin (generally under a few feet in thickness) leucocratic granitic pegmatite dikes. Most of these dikes contain abundant pink potassium feldspar, and contain biotite in their outer parts. The iron-titanium mineral ilmenite is a common accessory mineral.

The southern terminus of this unit is a complex fault zone, the Banning fault, which juxtaposes the gneiss with a varied assemblage of late Cenozoic-age sedimentary units to the south. All but one of these sedimentary units are of nonmarine origin. The oldest of the sedimentary deposits, termed the Hathaway Formation (Vaughan, 1922) is of early Pliocene age. This unit is discontinuously exposed between thrust faults within the Banning fault zone from the San Gorgonio River on the west, eastward to just east of Lion Canyon. This formation consists of a lower stratigraphic section exposed in the vicinity of Lion Canyon, and a more extensive upper section exposed in the area of Lion Canyon and Deep Canyon and further west in the

Hathaway Canyon area, from which this formation takes its name. The lower section consists of gray, well-indurated sandstone, with lesser amounts of siltstone, conglomerate, and local nonmarine limestone beds. The upper section is a moderately to well-indurated coarse-cobble to boulder conglomerate. Clasts are basement rocks of mixed composition, but cataclastic-texture lithologies are a predominant type. The Hathaway Formation is overlain on the east side of Lion Canyon by the Imperial Formation (Bramkamp, 1934; Vaughan, 1927; Allen, 1957). The Imperial Formation, of Pliocene age, is of marine origin and was deposited when the Gulf of California extended into the San Gorgonio Pass area, considerably north of its present northern terminus. The Imperial Formation consists of a sequence of brown to tan fine-grained sandstone and siltstone with thin gypsum beds. Marine invertebrate fossils are common within the Imperial Formation.

Overlying the Imperial Formation is the Painted Hills Formation, a thick section of nonmarine sandstone and conglomerate with both interbedded basalt flows and crosscutting basalt dikes. The Painted Hills Formation (Allen, 1957) of Pliocene age (?) is discontinuously exposed along the length of the reservation within the Banning fault zone. This nonmarine unit consists of moderately well-indurated gray conglomerate and conglomeratic sandstone. Interbedded with and intrusive into the Painted Hills Formation are flows and dikes of black olivine basalt. A large outcrop of basalt is located between Deep Canyon and Millard Canyon.

A small occurrence of the San Timoteo Formation, of Pliocene(?) age, is located between San Gorgonio River and Hathaway Creek (Allen, 1957). This unit, named for the San Timoteo Badlands southwest of the reservation, consists of moderately well-indurated, grayish, poorly bedded sandstone and conglomeratic sandstone.

The Cabezon Conglomerate (Vaughan, 1922), of late Tertiary or early Quaternary age, is a widespread sedimentary unit exposed along the southern edge of the mountains from the east edge of the reservation westward to Millard Canyon. The Cabezon Conglomerate consists of reddish, moderately well-indurated, poorly bedded fanglomerate. Unlike most of the other sedimentary units, the clasts in the Cabezon Conglomerate were locally derived.

Quaternary deposits of differing ages occur along the mountain front and along the major drainages. These consist mainly of unindurated to moderately indurated, poorly bedded conglomeratic sediments, all of local derivation. The older of these deposits are tannish to reddish in color and the younger grayish. The Pass area is covered by extensive alluvial-fan deposits emanating from the San Bernardino Mountains. These fan deposits are composed of mainly coarse cobbly alluvium. These extensive fan deposits have grown rapidly compared to those emanating from the San Jacinto Mountains to the south. This has resulted in forcing the San Gorgonio River against the high steep slopes at the base of the San Jacinto Mountains.

Landslides and landslide deposits are common north of San Gorgonio Pass. These landslides, generally possessing well-defined bounds, consist of rubbly rock material. Some older landslide deposits lack, or have considerably modified, landslide morphology. An extensive old landslide deposit is located south of Burro Flats and another east of Lion Canyon north of the Banning fault.

The reservation is crossed by the complex, east-striking Banning fault zone. This zone consists of a large number of north-dipping anastamosing thrusts. The larger of these contain thick layers of thoroughly brecciated rock and gouge layers which, at least locally, produce groundwater barriers. Dissected fault scarps occur along the southern part of the Banning fault zone, where they are located in intermediate age alluvium. The most obvious of these fault scarps is a sinuous scarp extending from Millard Canyon west to Potrero Creek. This fault, based upon the youthful appearance of the scarp, should be considered active.

The south branch of the northwest-striking seismically active San Andreas fault enters the reservation just west of Burro Flats and apparently joins the Banning fault zone in Potrero Creek. Prominent fault scarps along this fault are located along the west edge of Burro Flats.

South of the San Gorgonio Pass, the reservation parcels are underlain by near-equal amounts of granitic rock of the Southern California batholith and prebatholithic schist and gneiss.

The dark-gray schist and gneiss is mostly a well-layered biotite-rich schist occurring as masses of many sizes engulfed in granitic rock. The layering is produced principally by the varying amount of biotite to form biotite-rich layers alternating with layers largely devoid of biotite. Locally, non-foliated quartzite occurs within the schist. The schist commonly weathers to a reddish-colored soil, in contrast to the grayish soil derived from the granitic rocks.

The granitic rock, part of the Cretaceous-age Southern California batholith, includes tonalite, granodiorite, and quartz monzonite. Tonalite is the most common rock type. It is mainly gray, massive to foliated, medium-grained, sphene-bearing biotite-hornblende tonalite. In the southeastern (eastern part of sec. 24, T. 3 S., R. 2 E., S.B.M.), the tonalite is a very uniform-appearing massive sphene-rich biotite-hornblende tonalite which weathers to form large boulders of disintegration.

Locally, thin deposits of sandy gray unconsolidated alluvium occur in valley areas. A few landslides occur in these rocks along the steep northern front of the San Jacinto Mountains. A single northeast-striking unnamed fault is in the larger parcel of the reservation south of the San Gorgonio Pass.

Mineral Resources

No known mines or patented mining claims are on the Morongo Reservation, although deposits of tungsten, uranium, and limestone occur in adjacent areas. The only recorded mineral production on the reservation is from a peat deposit at Burro Flats (Saul, 1961) An unknown mineral prospect, not mentioned in the literature, is shown on the Lake Fulmor 7.5 minute quadrangle map in the SW¼ sec. 32, T. 3 S., R. 2 E. (Figure 51).

Tungsten

No tungsten deposits are known to exist on the reservation, although several tungsten mining claims occur very near reservation boundaries. The Blue Boy and Black Mountain claim groups are about a mile south of the reservation in sec. 3, T. 4 S., R. 1 E. (Figure 50). Scheelite occurs in a 2 to 4 ft-thick zone of calc-silicate rock. The Blue Boy Claims have produced 8 t of ore averaging 1 percent WO_3, and the Black Mountain Claims have produced 12 t of ore which assayed 6 percent WO_3 (Tucker and Sampson, 1941). The Blue Bird and Eagle Mining Claims, in sec. 29, T. 3 S., R. 1 E., are reported to be tungsten occurrences (Tucker and Sampson, 1945).

The tungsten deposits are associated with roof pendants of carbonate rock within the igneous-metamorphic complex of the northern San Jacinto Mountains. Similar rock types are likely to crop out on the Morongo Reservation and should be examined for possible tungsten mineralization.

Limestone

Roof pendants in igneous-metamorphic rocks in areas adjacent to the reservation contain large tonnages of intermixed high-calcium, low-iron limestone, dolomite, and magnesian limestone. These deposits are not developed at present, but appear promising for future development. They are close to rail and highway transportation and are among the few remaining undeveloped limestone deposits in southern California. Difficult access and environmental restrictions have hindered development (Bowen, 1957; Gray, 1973).

Limestone deposits adjacent to the Morongo Reservation include the Guiberson deposit, the Novelle deposit, and the Southern Pacific deposit (Tucker and Sampson, 1929, 1945; Logan, 1947; Oesterling and Spurk, 1964; Bowen and Gray,

1973). Tucker and Sampson (1929, p. 516) reported the following analysis of limestone from the Guiberson deposit:

```
Analysis in weight percent
SiO2               0.74
Al2O3              0.004
Fe2O3              0.008
CaO               53.29
MgO                2.39
```

This analysis, if representative of the deposit, indicates that the limestone is suitable for the manufacture of portland cement and agricultural lime.

Sand and Gravel

No sand and gravel deposits with recorded production are on the Morongo Indian Reservation. However, reservation land in the San Gorgonio Pass area probably contains sizable sand and gravel deposits. Three large deposits adjacent to the reservation are currently being exploited. These are the Beaumont Concrete Company deposit (NE¼ sec. 18, T. 3 S., R. 2 E.), the San Gorgonio Rock Products deposit (NW¼ sec. 3, T. 3 S., R. 1 E.), and the Massey Sand and Rock Company deposit (SW¼ sec. 23, T. 3 S., R. 4 E.) (Goldman, 1968).

Peat

A currently inactive peat deposit exists on the Morongo Reservation at Burro Flats, about 5 mi north of Banning. Peat is composed of partially decomposed plant remains and is used mainly as a soil conditioner. The peat bog covers an area of 21 acres and has a maximum thickness of 16 ft, thinning to the north and west. Peat has been quarried from the deposit in the past and marketed as a soil conditioner (Saul, 1961; U.S. Bureau of Mines, 1963).

Uranium and Thorium

No radioactive mineral deposits are known on the Morongo Reservation, but several deposits occur to the north in the San Bernardino Mountains. The St. Patrick Mining Claim Group, in the SW¼ sec. 8, T. 1 S., R. 1 E., about 5 mi northwest of the reservation boundary, is the closest radioactive mineral occurrence. Small crystals and grains of magnetite, allanite, uranothorite, and zircon occur in a 15 ft-thick lens of potassic feldspar, sodic plagioclase, quartz, and biotite in gneissic country rock (Dibblee, 1964). Radioactivity up to 45 times background count was measured at the deposit (Walker and others, 1956). A few tons of uranium ore were shipped from the claims in 1954 (Hewett and Stone, 1957).

The Thum Bum Claim, about 14 mi north of the reservation in sec. 28, T. 2 N., R. 2 E., produced 1,300 lb of ore assaying 0.20 percent U_3O_8. Radioactivity as high as 50 times background count occurs along a ¼ in. wide zone between Jurassic (?) granite and Precambrian (?) schist. An analysis of rock from the contact indicates the radioactivity is associated with crystals of altered zircon that contain thorium and some uranium (Walker and others, 1956).

Uranium and thorium potential of the Morongo Reservation is unknown, but granitic rocks, which may be possible sources of uranium and thorium, occur on the reservation in the San Bernardino and San Jacinto Mountains. Permeable sedimentary rocks, such as fanglomerates, which may serve as host rocks for secondary, leached uranium deposits, occur on the reservation in San Gorgonio Pass and surrounding foothills. A field investigation is required to assess the uranium and thorium potential.

Geothermal Resources

Geothermal resources of the Morongo Reservation are unknown. Numerous thermal springs and wells occur in the region, mostly related to fault systems (Waring, 1965). Highland Springs Resort, in the W½ sec. 25, T. 2 S., R. 1 W., 5 mi northwest of Banning, is the nearest thermal spring to the Morongo Reservation. Deeply circulating groundwater, with a temperature of 112° F., flows from springs along a portion of the San Andreas fault zone (Tucker and Sampson, 1945). A field study of the reservation should include a reconnaissance survey of well water temperatures.

Oil and Gas

No wells have been drilled for petroleum on the Morongo Reservation; however, at least 11 exploratory wells have been drilled within a 5 mi radius of the reservation. None of these wells encountered oil or gas (California Division of Oil and Gas, 1964; Munger, 1977).

Recommendations

A reconnaissance field study to determine the mineral potential of the reservation is recommended. The study should include a stream sediment sampling program, radiometric survey, and bulk sampling, beneficiation testing, and market analysis of possible limestone and sand and gravel deposits. Special attention should be given to locating and examining exposures of contact zones between carbonate rocks and igneous intrusions for tungsten mineralization.

SAN MANUEL INDIAN RESERVATION

Location

The San Manuel Indian Reservation is made up of sec. 20 and part of the N½NW¼ sec. 29, T. 1 N., R. 3 W., S.B.M., San Bernardino County, California (Figure 53). Total area of the reservation is 653 acres and the population is about 19 Indians. Tribal headquarters is in San Bernardino, near the southwest corner of the reservation.

The reservation is in the foothills of the San Bernardino Mountains and has a moderate climate. Elevations range from 1,440 ft to approximately 3,200 ft. The high relief makes access difficult and limits the potential usage of most of the reservation.

Geology

Most of the San Manuel Indian Reservation is underlain by gneiss of pre-Cretaceous age (Figure 54). Most of the gneiss is of biotite-feldspar-quartz composition. Layering is discontinuous and small-scale folds are common. Terminating the gneiss to the south is the north branch of the San Andreas fault zone, a wide complex fault zone.

South of the north branch of the San Andreas fault is a section of nonmarine Tertiary sediments of probable Miocene or Pliocene age (F. K. Miller, U.S. Geological Survey, unpublished mapping). Most of the sediments are brownish or reddish-brown, coarse-grained sandstone and conglomerate. The bedding, crude and thick, has an overall east strike and a consistent dip to the north. These sediments are terminated on the south by the south branch of the San Andreas fault.

Old, late Pleistocene or early Holocene unconsolidated alluvium of grayish to brownish color, occurs on both sides of Sand Canyon as extensive thick deposits and in the southeastern part of the reservation as several perched patches. An older (late Pleistocene or early Holocene) landslide deposit, overlain in part by older alluvium, occurs in the southeastern part of the reservation south of the north branch of the San Andreas fault. This deposit, terminated on the north by the fault, consists of poorly indurated rubble. Unconsolidated Holocene-age alluvium occurs along the bottom of Sand Canyon and in the prong of the reservation extending into the valley area. Several small landslides occur on the steep slopes underlain by the gneiss.

The San Andreas fault, which crosses the southern part of the reservation, is the master active fault in the western United States, capable of producing major to great earthquakes.

Mineral Resources

No mineral deposits are reported within the boundaries of the reservation. Sand Creek, which crosses the west side of the reservation, contains sand and gravel in its bed, as do all the streams in the area reaching the San Bernardino Valley. However, these deposits may not represent a potential mineral resource in this area because of the existence of much larger deposits nearby.

Arrowhead Hot Springs is about 2 mi northwest of the reservation. A resort hotel uses water from several springs for bathing, heating, and drinking (Waring, 1915). Temperatures of the springs range from 110° to 202° F.; total flow rate is estimated to be about 50 gal per minute (Waring, 1915). The springs appear to be associated with the San Andreas fault zone. Wells drilled on or near the San Andreas fault where it crosses the San Manuel Reservation might supply a source of hot water that could have potential value.

TWENTYNINE PALMS INDIAN RESERVATION

Location

The Twentynine Palms Reservation makes up the NW¼ sec. 4, T. 1 S., R. 9 E., S.B.M., Riverside County, California. Total area of the reservation, including a cemetery situated apart from the main reservation, is 162 acres. No Indians live on the reservation and tribal headquarters are in North Palm Springs, California. The reservation borders the town of Twentynine Palms on the northeast and Joshua Tree National Monument on the west (Figure 55). Terrain on the reservation is generally flat with a maximum relief of about 300 ft.

Geology

All but the southwestern part of the Twentynine Palms Indian Reservation is underlain by unconsolidated grayish coarse-grained alluvium of Quaternary age (Figure 56). The southwestern corner of the reservation is underlain by coarse-grained quartz-monzonite of Cretaceous age (Rogers, 1967).

Mineral Resources

No mineral resources are known to exist on the reservation. Most all the tribal land appears to be underlain by alluvial fan deposits at the surface and probably quartz-monzonite rock at depth (Rogers, 1958). The surface deposits may have some potential as a source of gravel if a nearby market is available.

SANTA YNEZ INDIAN RESERVATION

Location

The Santa Ynez Reservation is situated in Santa Barbara County, California, about 32 mi northwest of Santa Barbara, and 3 mi east of the small town of Solvang, California. State Highway 150 passes near the reservation. In 1971, 42 Indians resided on or adjacent to the reservation.

The reservation consists of 99.28 acres of land in a narrow strip along Zanja de Cota Creek on unsurveyed portions of what would be sec. 12, 13, 24, T. 6 N., R. 31 W. and sec. 7, T. 6 N., R. 30 W. (Figure 57). Relief is low, with mean elevations around 500 ft. The environment of the reservation includes rolling hills, trees, a year-round stream, and a mild climate. Temperature extremes are 97° and 47° F., and annual rainfall is about 8 in.

Geology

The Santa Ynez Indian Reservation is underlain by unconsolidated Quaternary age terrace deposits along Zanja de Cota Creek (Dibblee, 1950).

Mineral Resources

Because of its relatively small size and surface cover of Quaternary terrace deposits, the mineral potential of the Santa Ynez Reservation is unknown. Tertiary sedimentary formations that have produced oil and gas elsewhere appear to underlie the terrace deposits on the reservation.

In the Zaca Field, which is about 10 miles to the northwest, oil is produced from fractured cherty shale of the Monterey Formation where it underlies the Sisquoc Formation. These same formations form an anticlinal structure beneath the Santa Ynez Reservation (Dibblee, 1950, pl. 4 and 5). The presence of oil or gas within the inferred trap can be determined only by drilling.

Diatomite occurs in outcrops about 3 mi east and 3 mi west of the reservation. Sand and gravel is produced from the Santa Ynez riverbed, a short distance south of the reservation.

CONCLUSIONS AND RECOMMENDATIONS

The only established mining district on tribal lands in Southern California is on the Pala Indian Reservation. The Pala mining district dates from the 1890's and was the most important source of lithium in the United States during the early part of this century. The district is also a world-renowned source of semiprecious gemstones. Other tribal lands that border or overlap gem- and lithium-bearing pegmatite resources are the Pechanga, Pauma-Yuima, Rincon, La Jolla, San Pasqual, Santa Ysabel, Mesa Grande, Inaja-Cosmit, and Ramona Indian Reservations. In view of the present demand and high prices for semiprecious gemstones and the potential increase in demand for lithium, it is recommended that a field reconnaissance study be carried out on these reservations. The study should include the location and mapping of pegmatite exposures, analysis of selected rock samples, and geochemical sampling of streams, springs, and wells. In addition, an economic appraisal should be made of potential resources of dimension stone and sand and gravel.

The Santa Ysabel, Inaja-Cosmit, Cuyapaipe, La Posta, Manzanita, Los Coyotes, and Santa Rosa Indian Reservations are located adjacent to previously active gold and tungsten mining districts. Tribal lands are underlain by rocks that may also contain these commodities. For this reason, geochemical sampling of stream sediments and soils on these reservations is recommended. The Barona Reservation contains a reported gold deposit and is located adjacent to a developed copper mine. The gold deposit and any extensions of the adjacent copper-bearing zone should be examined in conjunction with a geochemical sampling program.

Because most of the tribal lands in Southern California were set aside near the end of the past century, it is very likely that little or no prospecting has been carried out during this century on large segments of the reservations. Therefore, it is recommended that reconnaissance investigations be made of the Capitan Grande, Los Coyotes, Cahuilla, Morongo, and Agua Caliente Reservations, all of which contain large areas of uninhabited terrain. In addition, the Torres Martinez and possibly the Agua Caliente Reservations have potential for geothermal resources and warrant further geophysical and geochemical investigations.

REFERENCES

Berman, E. R., 1975, Geothermal Energy: Park Ridge, New Jersey, Noyes Data Corporation, 336 p.

Blake, R. L., 1974, Extracting minerals from geothermal brines: A literature study: U.S. Bureau of Mines Information Circular 8638, 25 p.

Bowen, O. E., Jr., 1957, Cement: in Wright, L. A., ed., Mineral commodities of California: California Division of Mines Bulletin 176, p. 113-120.

Bowen, O. E., Jr., and Gray, C. H., 1973, Deposits particularly promising for near-future development: in Bowen, O. E., Jr., ed., Limestone and dolomite resources of California: California Division of Mines and Geology Bulletin 194, chap. 5, p. 46-48.

California Division of Mines and Geology, 1942, Mines and mineral deposits in Riverside County: California Journal Mines and Geology, v. 38, p. 344.

____,1968, Mines and mineral deposits in Riverside County: California Division of Mines and Geology, unpublished report, 1,636 p.

California Division of Oil and Gas, 1964, Exploratory wells drilled outside of oil and gas fields in California to December 31, 1963: San Francisco, California Division of Oil and Gas, 320 p.

Creasey, S. C., 1946, Geology and nickel mineralization of the Julian Cuyamaca area, San Diego County, California: California Journal of Mines and Geology, v. 42, no. 1, p. 15-29.

Dibblee, T. W., Jr., 1950, Geology of the southwestern Santa Barbara County, California: California Division of Mines Bulletin 150, 95 p.

____,1964, Geologic map of the San Gorgonio Mountain Quadrangle, San Bernardino and Riverside Counties, California: U.S. Geological Survey Miscellaneous Geological Investigations Map I-431, scale 1:62,500.

Dietrich, W. F., 1928, The clay resources and the ceramic industry of California: California Mineral Bureau Bulletin 99, 383 p.

Donnelly, M., 1934, Geology and mineral deposits of the Julian District, San Diego County, California: California Division of Mines Bulletin 30, no. 4, p. 331-370.

Ellis, A. J., and Lee, C. H., 1919, Geology and ground waters of the western part of San Diego County, California: U.S. Geological Survey, Water Supply Paper 446, 321 p.

Ellsberg, Helen, 1972, Mines of Julian: Glendale, California, La Siesta Press, 71 p.

Everhard, D. L., 1951, Geology of the Cuyamaca Peak Quadrangle, San Diego County, California: California Division of Mines Bulletin 159, p. 51-116.

Ford, W. E., 1906, Some interesting beryl crystals and their associations: American Journal of Science, v. 22, p. 221.

Frazer, D. M., 1931, Geology of the San Jacinto Quadrangle, south of San Gorgonio Pass: California Division of Mines, 27th Report of State Mineralogist, p. 494-540.

Goldman, H. B., 1968, Sand and gravel in California: An inventory of deposits, Southern California: California Division of Mines and Geology Bulletin 180-C, Part C, 56 p.

Hanley, J. B., 1951, Economic geology of the Rincon pegmatites, San Diego County, California: California Division of Mines Special Report 7-B, 24 p.

Hewett, D. F., and Stone, J., 1957, Uranothorite near Forest Home, San Bernardino County, California: American Mineralogist, v. 42, p. 104-107.

Hornburg, C. D., 1977, Geothermal development of the Salton Sea: Chemical Engineering Progress, July, v. 73, p. 89-94.

Hubon, I. A., 1902, Register of mines and minerals, San Diego County, California: California Mineral Bureau, 11 p.

Irwin, W. P., Greene, R. C., and Thurber, H. K., 1970, Mineral resources of the Agua Tibia Primitive Area, California: U.S. Geological Survey Bulletin 1319-A, 19 p.

Jahns, R. H., 1979, Gem-bearing pegmatites in San Diego County: in Abbott, P. L., and Todd, V. R., eds., Mesozoic crystalline rocks: San Diego State University, Department of Geological Science, p. 1-38.

Jahns, R. H., and Wright, L. A., 1951, Gem and lithium-bearing pegmatites of the Pala district, San Diego County, California: California Division of Mines Special Report 7-A, 70 p.

Kennedy, M. P., 1977, Recency and character of faulting along the Elsinore fault zone in southern Riverside County, California: California Division of Mines and Geology Special Report 131, 12 p.

Kunz, G. F., 1903, Native bismuth and bismite from Pala, California: American Journal of Science, v. 16, p. 398-399.

____, 1905, Gems, jewelers' materials and ornamental stones of California: California Minerals Bureau Bulletin 37, 171 p.

Larsen, E. S., Jr., 1948, Batholith and associated rocks of Corona, Elsinore, and San Luis Rey Quadrangles, southern California: Geological Society of America Memoir 29, 182 p.

Lofgren, B. E., 1976, Land subsidence and aquifer-system compaction in the San Jacinto Valley, Riverside County, California--a progress report: U.S. Geological Survey Journal Research, v. 4, p. 9-18.

Logan, C. A., 1947, Limestone in California: California Journal of Mines and Geology, v. 43, p. 175-357.

Mann, J. F., 1955, Geology of a portion of the Elsinore fault zone, California: California Division of Mines and Geology Special Report 43, 22 p.

Merriam, R., 1946, Igneous and metamorphic rocks of the southwestern part of the Ramona Quadrangle, San Diego County, California: Geological Society of America Bulletin, v. 57, p. 223-260.

____, 1951, Groundwater in the bedrock in western San Diego County, California: California Division of Mines Bulletin 159, p. 117-128.

____, 1958, Geology of the Santa Ysabel Quadrangle, San Diego County, California: California Division of Mines Bulletin 177, p. 7-20.

Merrill, F. J., 1917, Riverside County: California Mineral Bureau, Report 15 of the State Mineralogist, p. 522-582.

Mining Engineering, 1979, "Thar's gold in them thar wells'": v. 31, p. 146-147.

Morton, P. K., 1977, Geology and mineral resources of Imperial County: California Division of Mines and Geology County Report 7, 104 p.

Moyle, W. R., Jr., 1976, Geohydrology of the Anza-Terwilliger area, Riverside County, California: U.S. Geological Survey Water Resources Investigations 76-10 (NTIS Report PB 252 834), 25 p.

Munger, A. H., ed., 1977, California-Alaska oil and gas fields: Los Angeles, Munger Map Book Company.

Murdoch, J., and Webb, R. W., 1948, Minerals of California: California Division of Mines Bulletin 136.

____, 1956, Minerals of California: California Division Mines Bulletin 173, 452 p.

Oesterling, W. A., and Spurk, W. H., 1964, Eastern Mojave and Colorado Deserts; in Minerals for industry: San Francisco, Southern Pacific Company, v. 3, pt. 3, p. 99-198.

Olmstead, F. H., 1953, Geologic features and water resources of Campo, Mesa Grande, La Jolla, and Pauma Indian Reservation, San Diego County, California: U.S. Geological Survey Administrative Report, 126 p.

Robinson, P. T., Elders, W. A., and Muffler, L.J.P., 1976, Quaternary volcanism in the Salton Sea geothermal field, Imperial Valley, California: Geological Society of America Bulletin, v. 87, p. 347-360.

Rogers, A. F., 1910, Minerals from the pegmatite veins of Rincon, San Diego County, California: Columbia University School of Mines Quarterly, v. 31, p. 208-218.

Rogers, J.J.W., 1958, Textural and spectrochemical studies of the White Tank quartz monzonite, California: Geological Society of America Bulletin, v. 69, p. 449-464.

Rogers, T. H., compiler, 1965, Geologic map of California, Santa Ana sheet: California Division of Mines and Geology, scale 1:250,000.

____, 1967, San Bernardino sheet: California Division of Mines and Geology, Geologic Map of California, scale 1:250,000.

Saul, R. B., 1961, New peat deposit: California Division of Mines and Geology Mineral Information Service, v. 14, no. 10, p. 8-9.

Schaller, W. T., 1905, Dumortierite: U.S. Geological Survey Bulletin 262, p. 91-120.

Sharp, R. V., 1967, San Jacinto fault zone in the Peninsula Ranges of southern California: Geological Society of America Bulletin, v. 78, p. 705-730.

Singer, J. A., 1979, Water resources of the Santa Ynez Indian Reservation, Santa Barbara County, California: U.S. Geological Survey Open-File report 79-413, 27 p.

Singleton, R. H., 1979, Lithium: U.S. Bureau of Mines Mineral Commodity Profile, 25 p.

Sinkankas, J., 1976, Gemstones of North America: New York, Van Nostrand, v. 2, 494 p.

Stewart, R. M., 1958, Mines and mineral resources of Santa Ysabel Quadrangle, San Diego County, California: California Division of Mines Bulletin 177, p. 21-42.

Swanberg, C. A., 1976, Mesa geothermal anomaly, Imperial Valley, California: Second U. N. Symposium on the Development and Use of Geothermal Resources, Proceedings, v. 2, p. 1217-1230.

Thrush, P. W., 1968, A dictionary of mining, mineral and related terms: U.S. Bureau of Mines, 1269 p.

Todd, V. R., 1978, Geologic map of the Viejas Mountain 7.5' quadrangle, San Diego County, California: U.S. Geological Survey Open-File Report 78-113, scale 1:24,000

____, 1979, Geology of the Mount Laguna 7.5' quadrangle, San Diego, California: U.S. Geological Survey Open-File Report 79-862, scale 1:24,000.

Todd, V. R., 1980, Geology of the Alpine 7.5' quadrangle, San Diego County, California: U.S. Geological Survey Open-File Report 80-82, scale 1:24,000.

Tucker, W. B., 1921, San Diego County, California: California Minerals Bureau Report 17, p. 264-390.

____, 1924, San Diego County, California: California Minerals Bureau Report 20, p. 368-374.

____, 1925, San Diego County, California: California Minerals Bureau Report 21, p. 325-382.

Tucker, W. B., and Sampson, R. J., 1929, Los Angeles field division--Riverside County: California Division of Mines Report 25, p. 468-526.

____, 1941, Recent developments in the tungsten resources of California: California Journal of Mines and Geology, v. 37, p. 565-588.

____, 1945, Mineral resources of Riverside County, California Journal of Mines and Geology, v. 41, p. 121-182.

U.S. Bureau of Mines, 1963, Minerals Yearbook, 1962: v. 3, Area reports, p. 212.

U.S. Department of Commerce, 1974, Federal and State Indian Reservations and Indian trust areas: Washington, D. C., U.S. Government Printing Office, 604 p.

VerPlanck, W. E., 1958, Salt in California: California Division of Mines Bulletin 175, 168 p.

Walker, G. W., Lovering, T. G., and Stephens, H. G., 1956, Radioactive deposits in California: California Division of Mines Special Report 49, 38 p.

Waring, G. A., 1905, Quartz from San Diego County, California: American Journal of Science, v. 20, p. 125-127.

____, 1915, Springs of California: U.S. Geological Survey Water Supply Paper 338, 410 p.

____, 1965, Thermal springs of the United States and other countries of the world, revised by R. R. Blankenship and Ray Bentall: U.S. Geological Survey Professional Paper 492, 383 p.

Weber, F. H., Jr., 1963, San Diego County: California Division of Mines and Geology County Report 3, 309 p.

Wright, L. A., 1946, Geology of the Santa Rosa Mountain area, Riverside County, California: California Journal of Mines and Geology, v. 42, p. 9-13.

____, 1957, Gemstones, in Mineral commodities of California: California Division of Mines Bulletin 176, p. 205-214.

Click back button (<<) on toolbar to return to text

Table 1.--Mines and mineral occurrences in the vicinity of the Santa Rosa Indian Reservation

Property name	Location	Commodity	Reference	Occurrences
Winchester	NW1/4SW1/4SE1/4 sec. 29, T. 6 S., R. 4 E.	Gold	Calif. Div. Mines (1968) unpub. rept., Riverside County	
Renrut-Neery	SE1/4SE1/4SW1/4 sec. 29, T. 6 S., R. 4 E.	Gold	Tucker and Sampson (1945), plate 35	
Hemet Belle	sec. 31, T. 6 S., R. 4 E.	Gold	Merrill (1917, p. 535)	Quartz veins in gneiss at contact with granite.
Minnie Ha-Ha	N1/2NE1/4NW1/4 sec. 32, T. 6 S., R. 4 E.	Gold	Calif. Div. Mines (1968) unpub. rept., Riverside County	
Gold Shot	secs. 28, 29, and 33 T. 6 S., R. 4 E.	Gold	Tucker and Sampson (1945)	Quartz veins in granite with limestone roof pendants.
Big Cat Mine	SW1/4SW1/4SW1/4 sec. 17, T. 7 S., R. 4 E.	Gold	U.S. Bureau of Mines, MILS files	
Oro Vista Mine	sec. 28, T. 7 S., R. 5 E.	Gold	Tucker and Sampson (1945)	Quartz veins at contact between granite and schist.
Garnet Queen Mine	sec. 20, T. 7 S., R. 5 E.	Tungsten	Tucker and Sampson (1945)	Scheelite ore in tactite at contact between granite and schist.
Indian Mine	sec. 28, T. 7 S., R. 5 E.	Tungsten	Tucker and Sampson (1945)	Scheelite ore in tactite.
Milkyway Claims	secs. 26 and 27, T. 7 S., R. 5 E.	Tungsten	Calif. J. Mines and Geology (1942)	

Continued

Click back button (<<) on toolbar to return to text

Table 1.--Mines and mineral occurrences in the vicinity of the Santa Rosa Indian Reservation

Property name	Location	Commodity	Reference	Occurrences
Ribbonwood Tungsten	sec. 26, T. 7 S., R. 5 E.	Tungsten	Tucker and Sampson (1945)	Scheelite ore in tactite at contact between granite and schist.
Whitlock	secs. 27, 28, and 34, T. 6 S., R. 4 E.	Limestone	Calif. Div. Mines (1968) unpub. rept., Riverside County.	
Harris	sec. 9, T. 7 S., R. 5 E.	Limestone	Logan (1947).	
Nightingale	secs. 6, 8, 9, 10, 11, and 12, T. 7 S., R. 5 E.	Limestone	Calif. Div. Mines (1968) unpub. rept., Riverside County.	
Charleroix (Percival)	secs. 29 and 32, T. 6 S., R. 5 E.	Asbestos	Calif. Div. Mines (1968) unpub. rept., Riverside County.	
Unnamed prospect	sec. 31, T. 7 S., R. 6 E.	Asbestos	Murdoch and Webb (1956).	
Unnamed prospect	sec. 4 and 5, T. 7 S. R. 6 E.	Asbestos	Merrill (1917).	
Charleboix	sec. 30, T. 7 S., R. 5 E.	Beryl	U.S. Bureau of Mines, MILS files.	
Santa Rosa Mountain	sec. 29, T. 7 S., R. 5 E.	Beryl	Calif. Div. Mines (1968) unpub. rept., Riverside County.	

Return to text

Click back button (<<) on toolbar to return to text

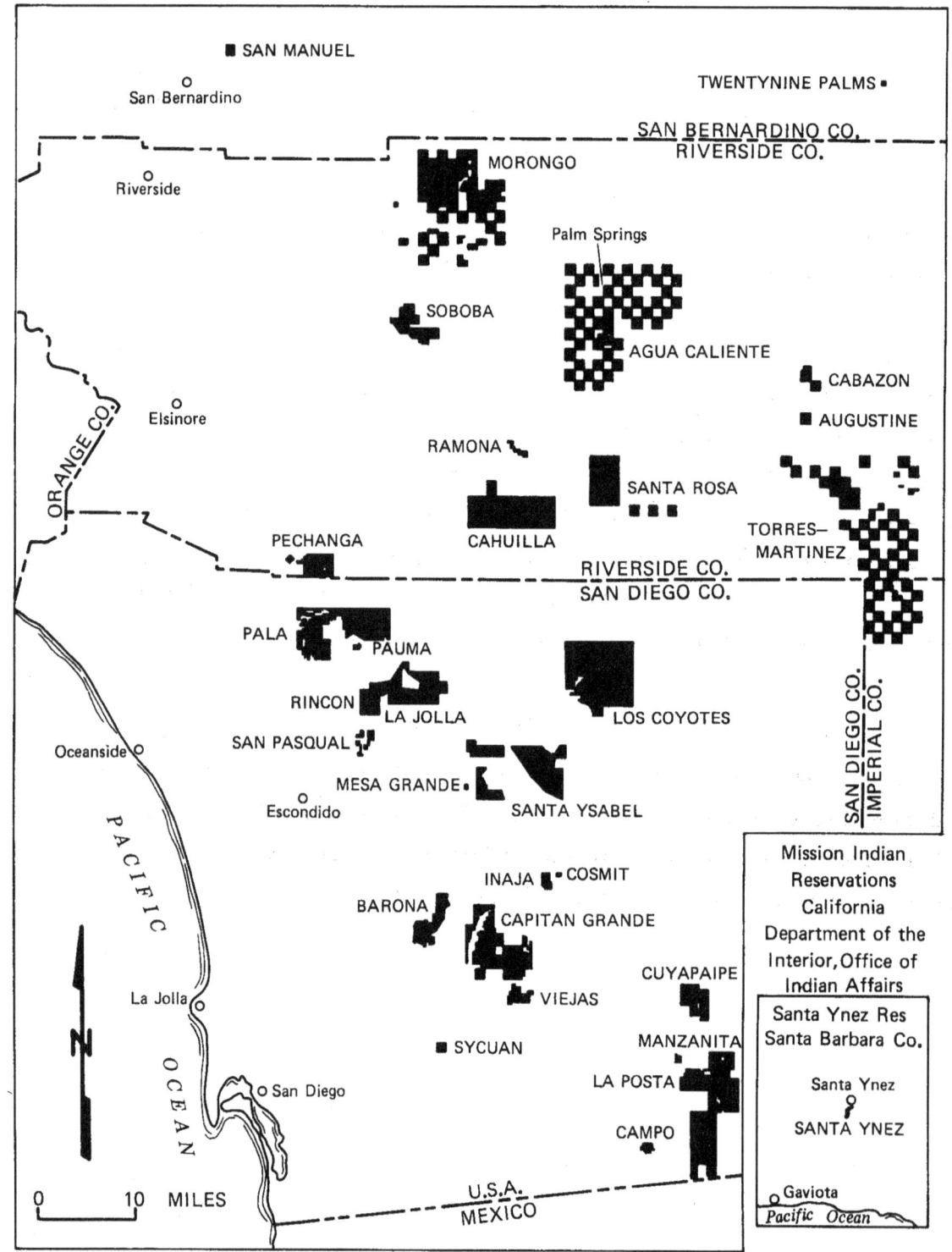

Figure 1. Mission Indian Reservations in Southern California.

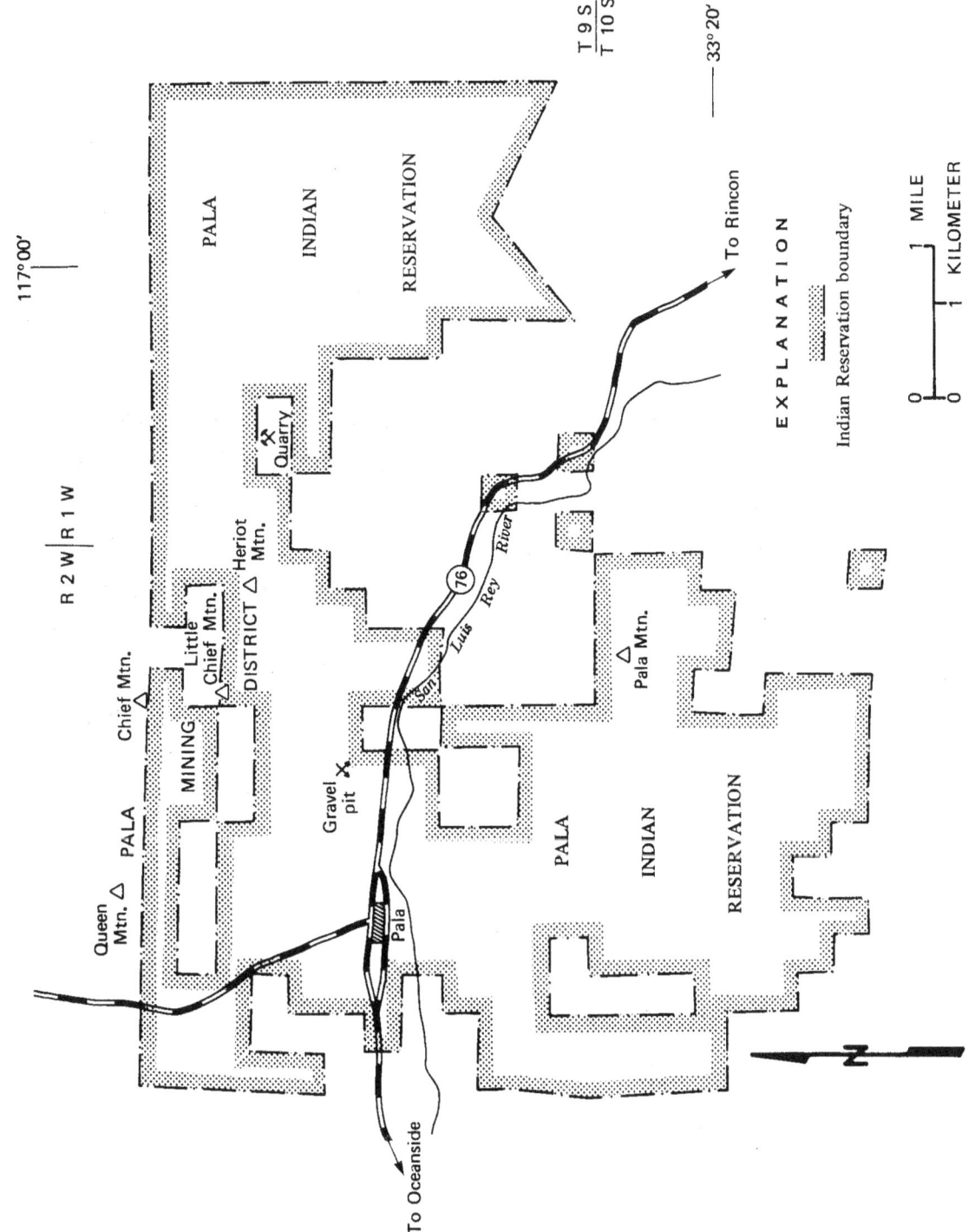

Figure 2. Mineral resource map of the Pala Indian Reservation.

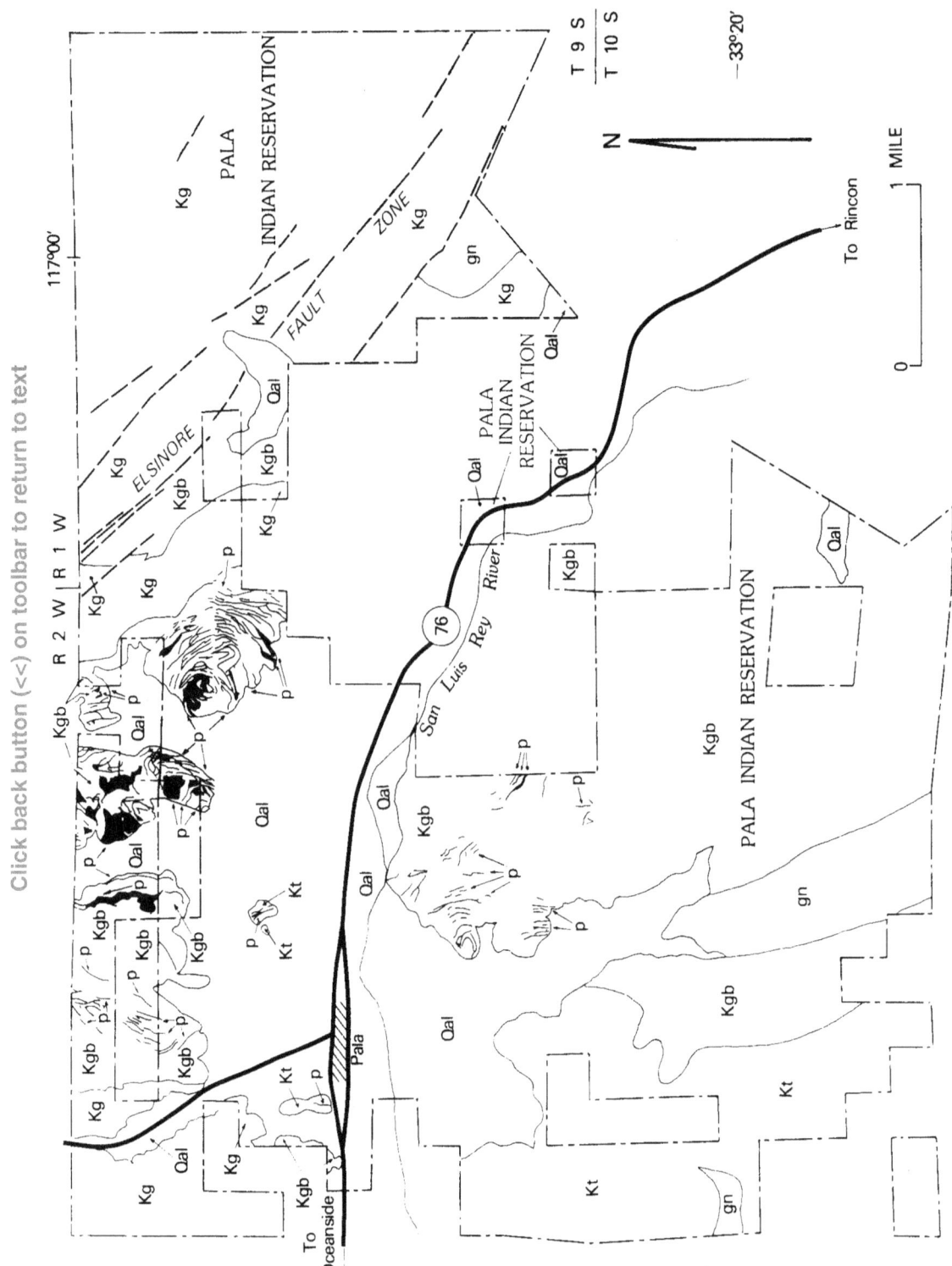

Figure 3. Geologic map of the Pala Indian Reservation (from Jahns and Wright, 1951; Weber, 1963). Quaternary alluvial deposits (Qal); granitic pegmatite dikes (p); granodiorite (Kg); tonalite (Kt); gabbro (Kgb); schist and gneiss (gn).

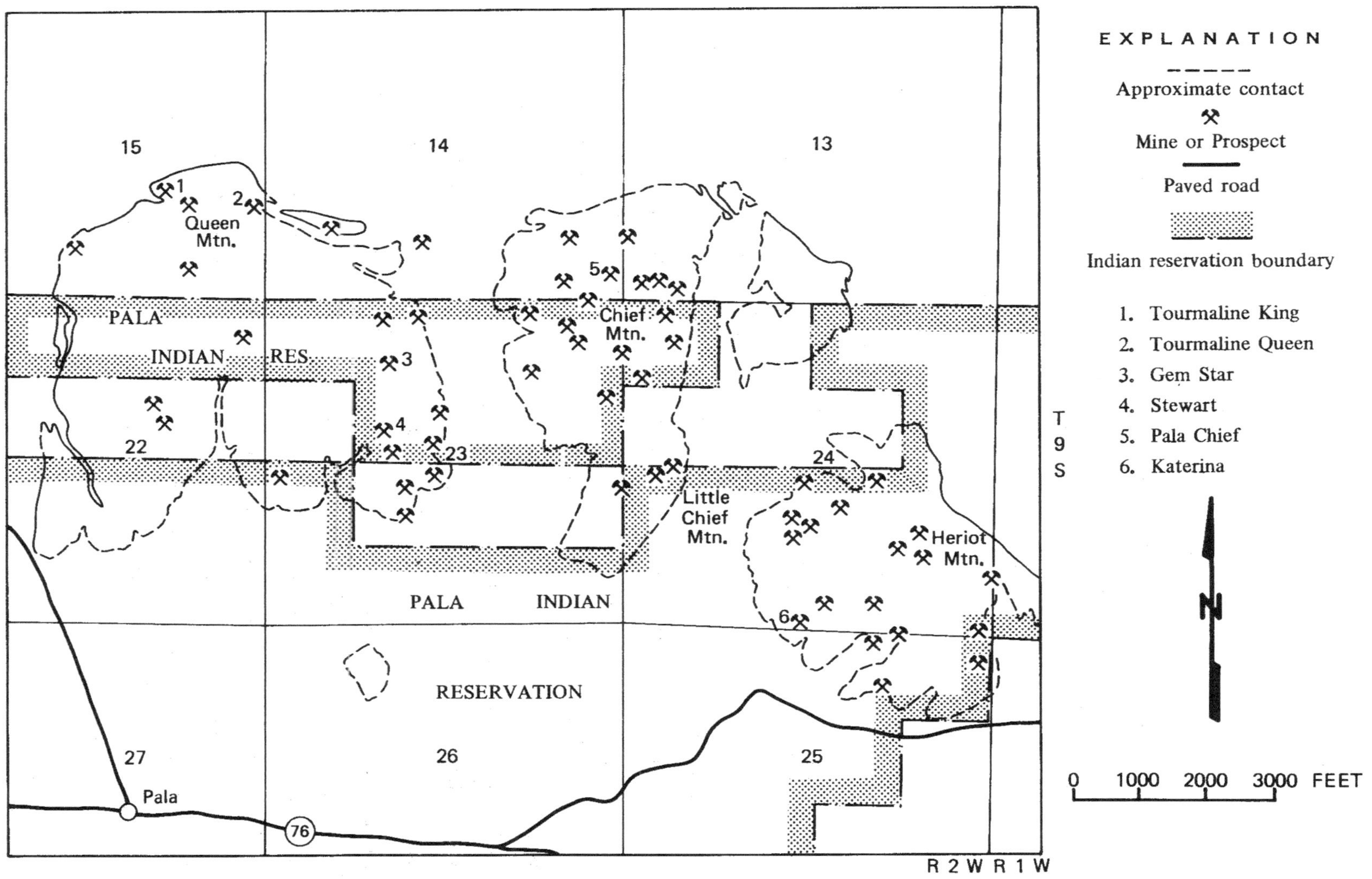

Figure 4. Mines and prospects of the Pala mining district.

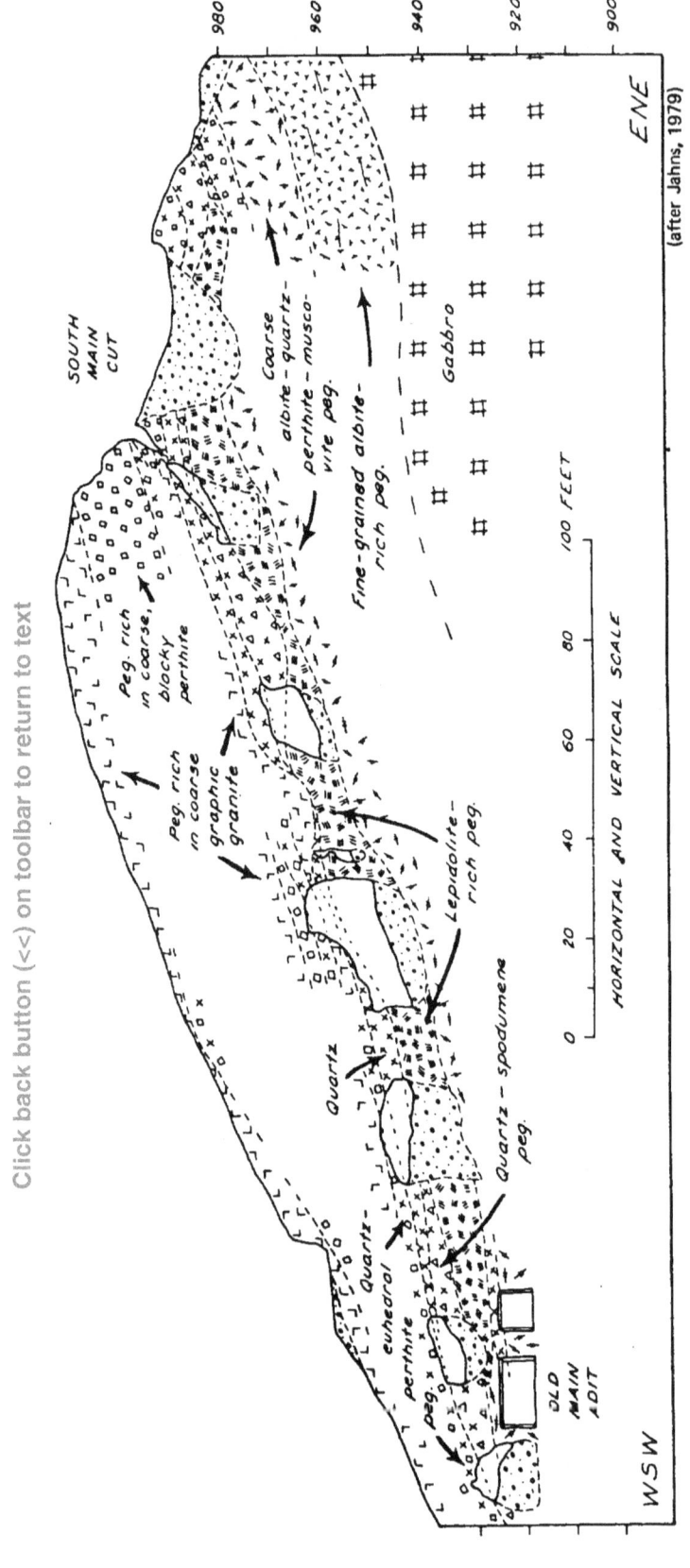

Figure 5. Geologic cross-section through part of the Stewart Mine.

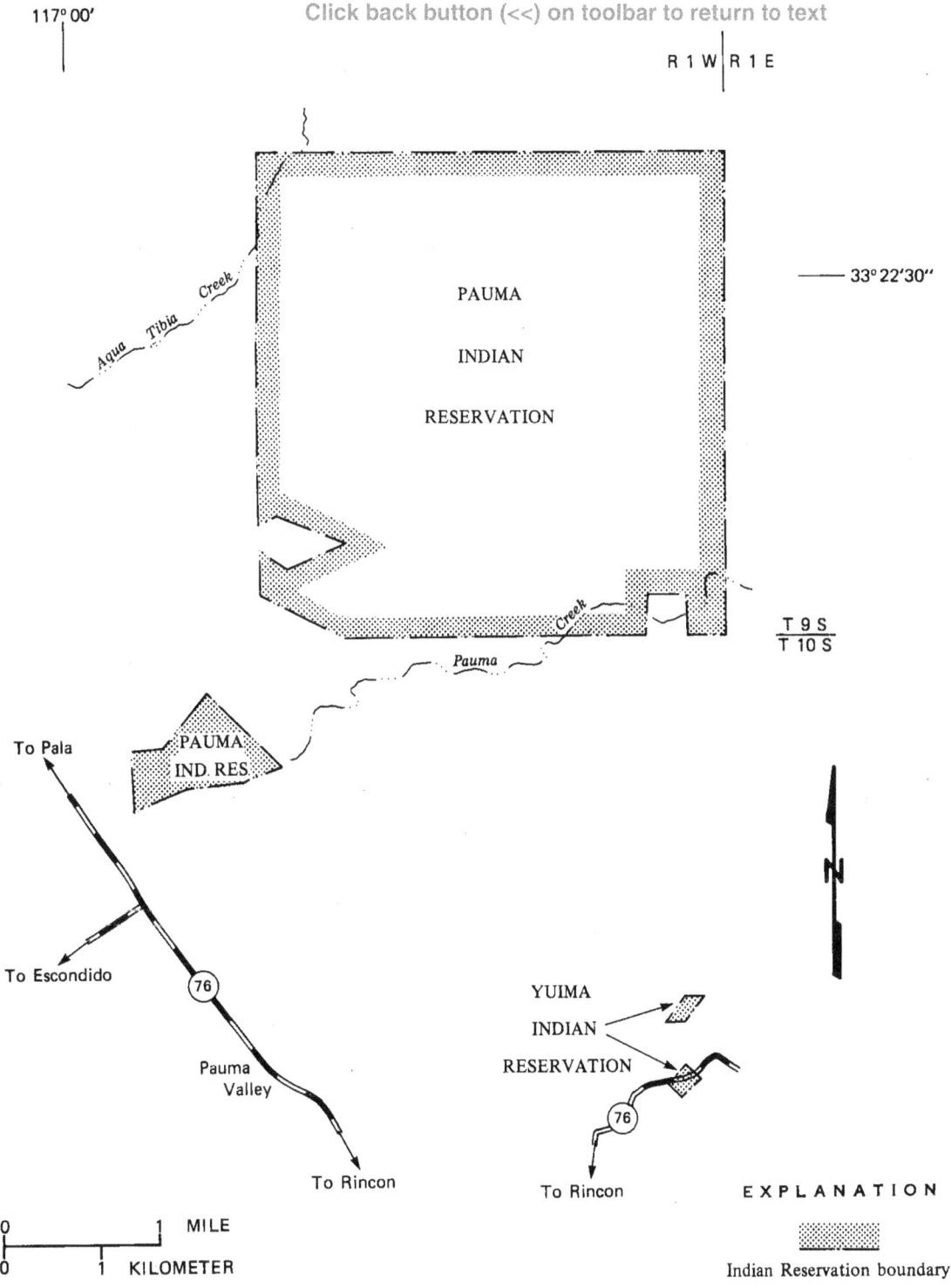

Figure 6. Mineral resource map of the Pauma and Yuima Indian Reservation.

Click back button (<<) on toolbar to return to text

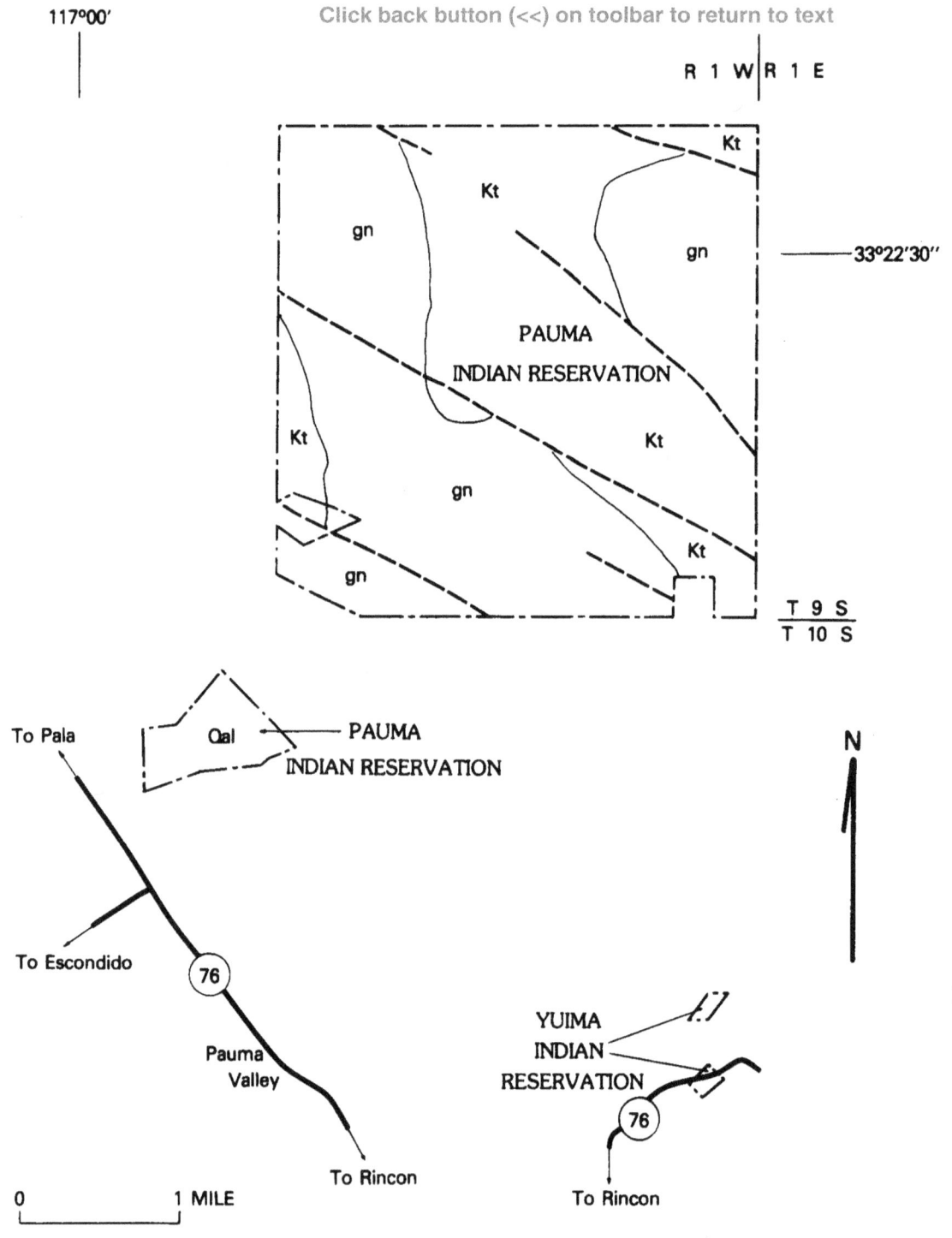

Figure 7. Geologic map of the Pauma Indian Reservation (from Weber, 1963). Quaternary alluvium (Qal); tonalite (Kt); schist and gneiss (gn).

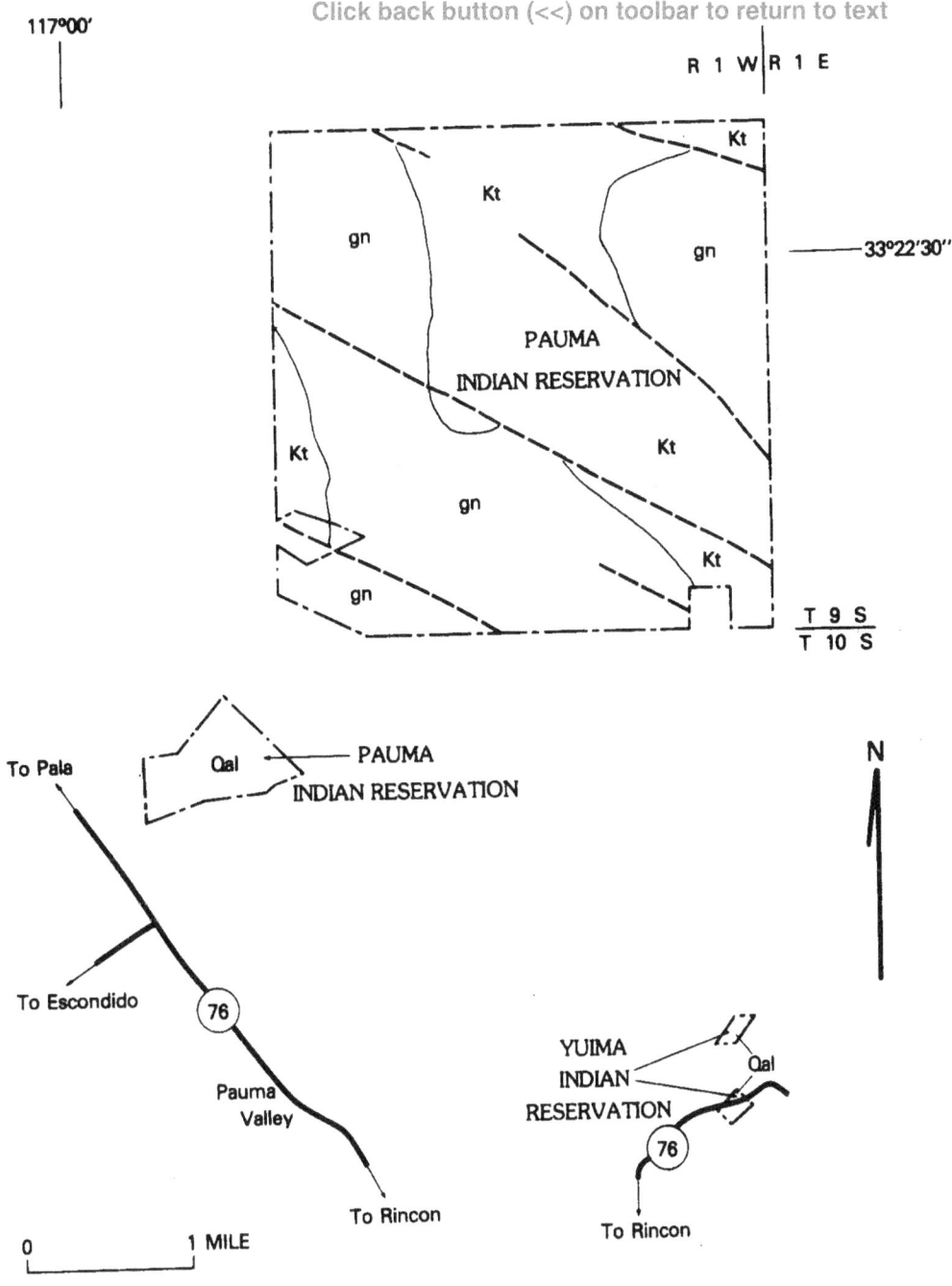

Figure 8. Geologic map of the Yuima Indian Reservation (from Weber, 1963). Quaternary alluvium (Qal).

Click back button (<<) on toolbar to return to text

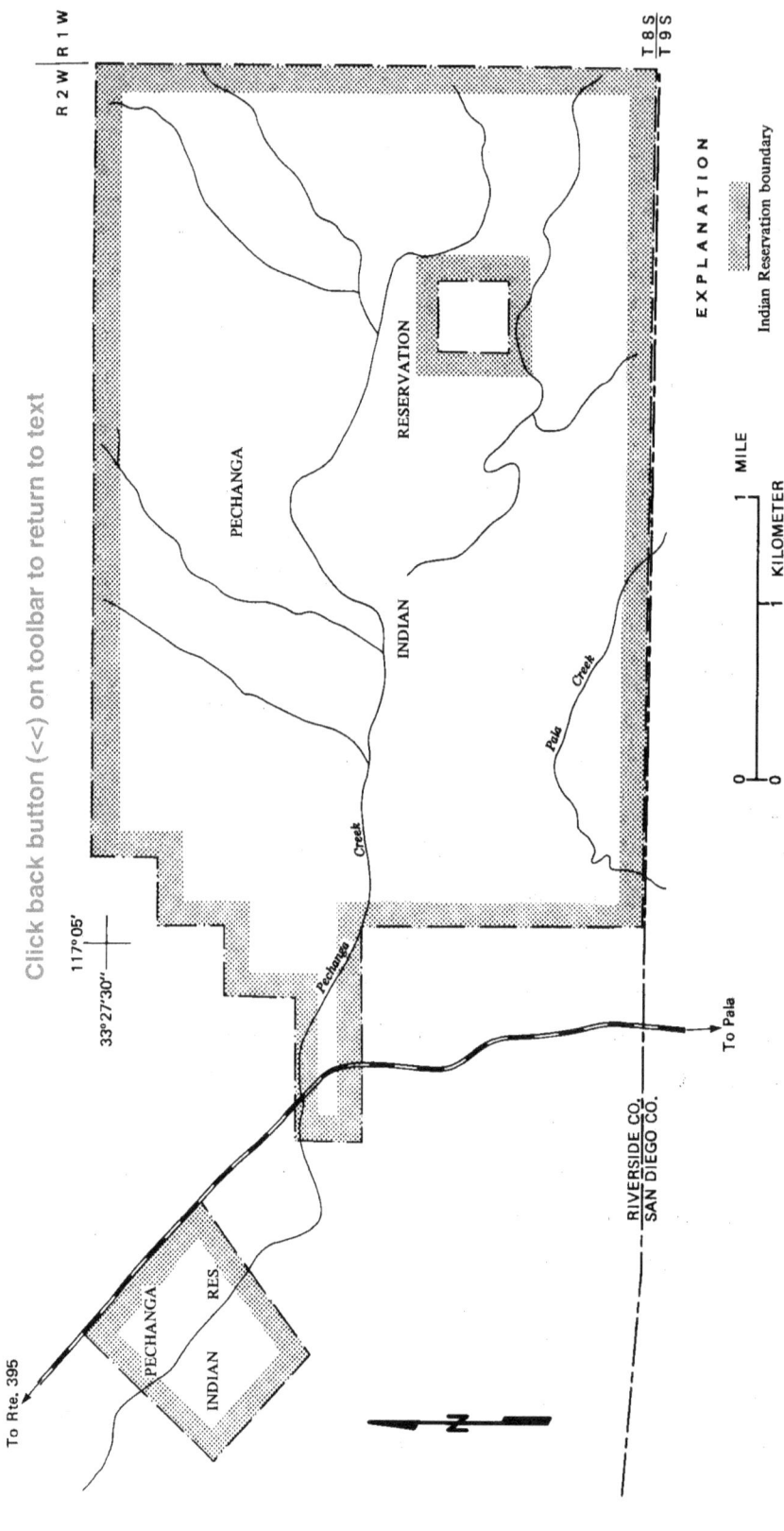

Figure 9. Mineral resource map of the Pechanga Indian Reservation.

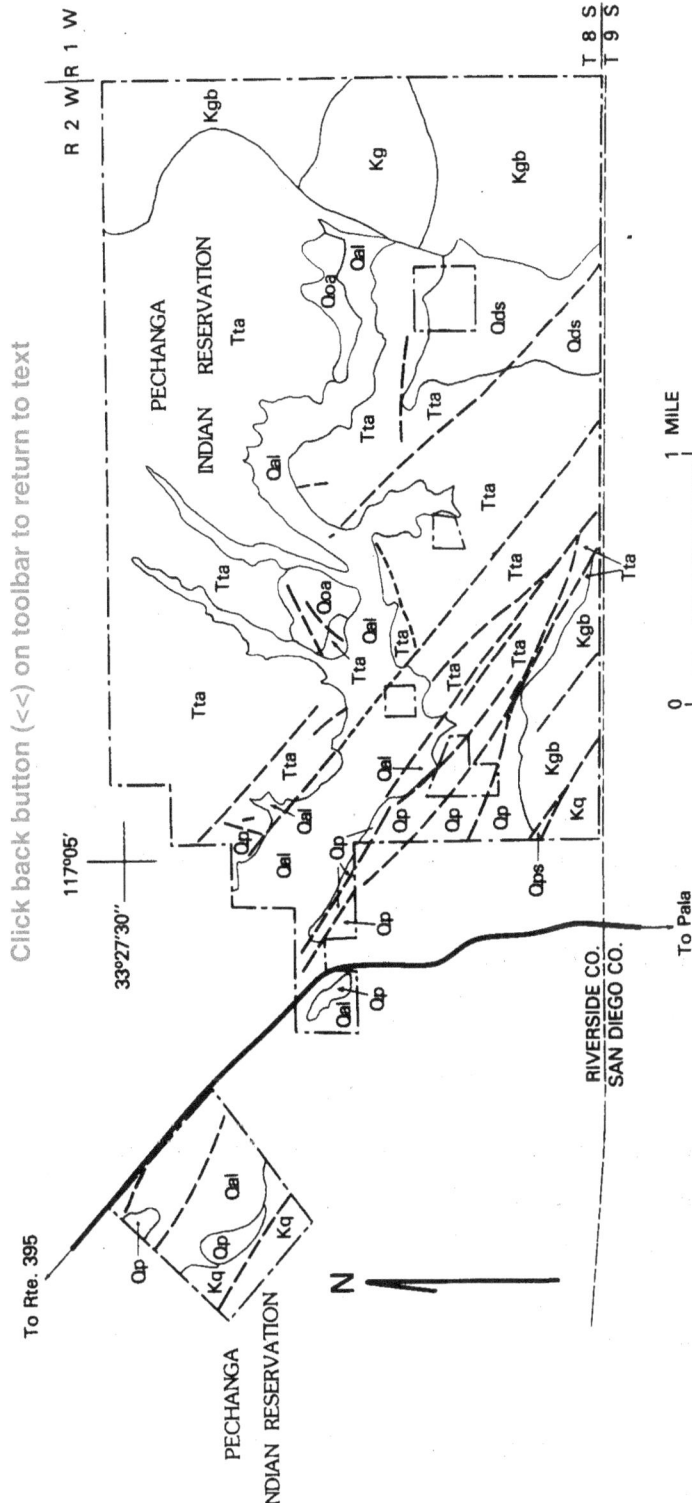

Figure 10. Geologic map of the Pechanga Indian Reservation (from Kennedy, 1977). Quaternary alluvium (Qal); older Quaternary terrace deposits (Qoa); Dripping Springs Formation (Qds); Pauba Formation (Qp); Temecula Arkose (Tta); quartz-monzonite (Kq); granodiorite (Kg); gabbro (Kgb).

Click back button (<<) on toolbar to return to text

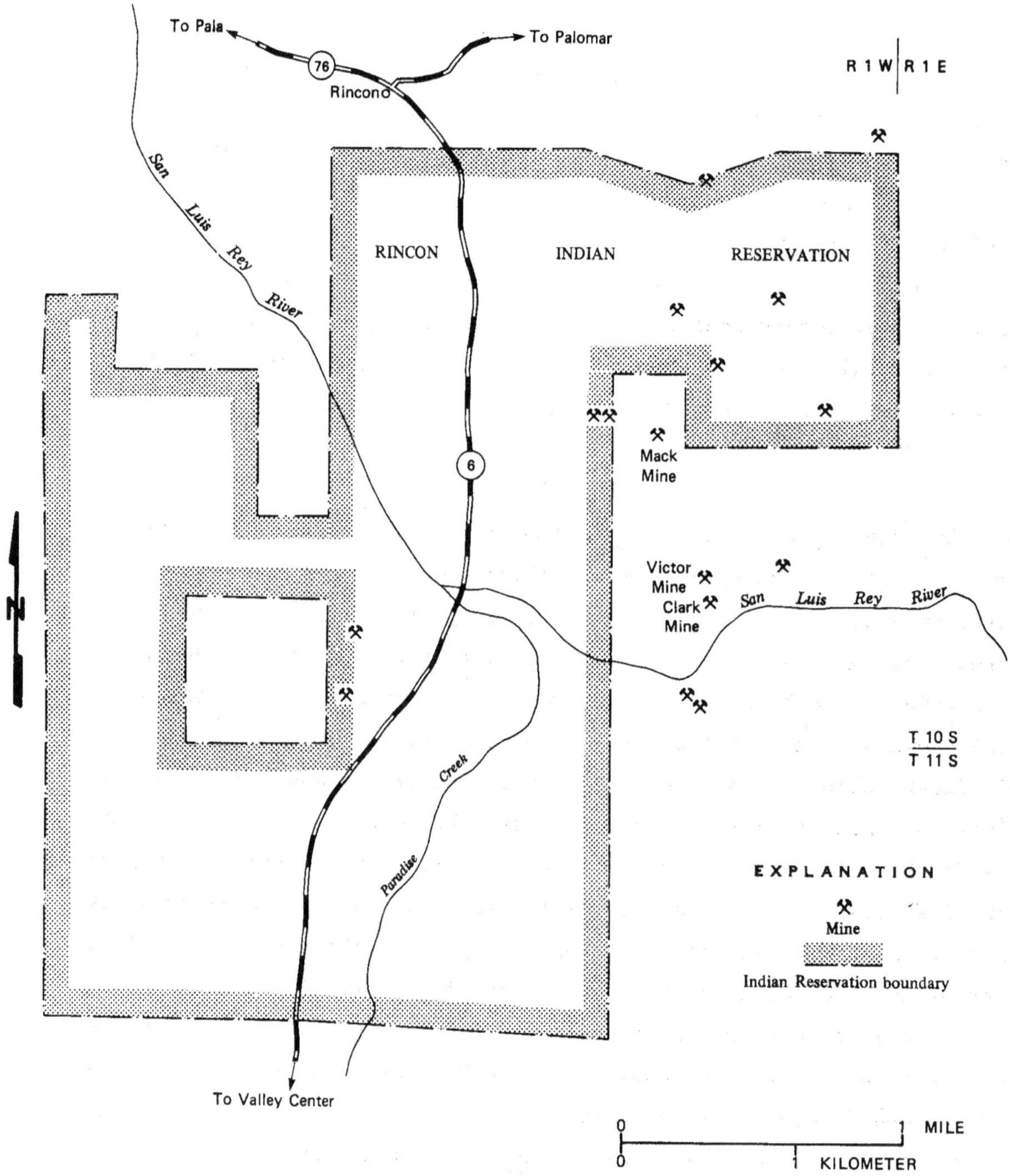

Figure 11. Mineral resource map of the Rincon Indian Reservation.

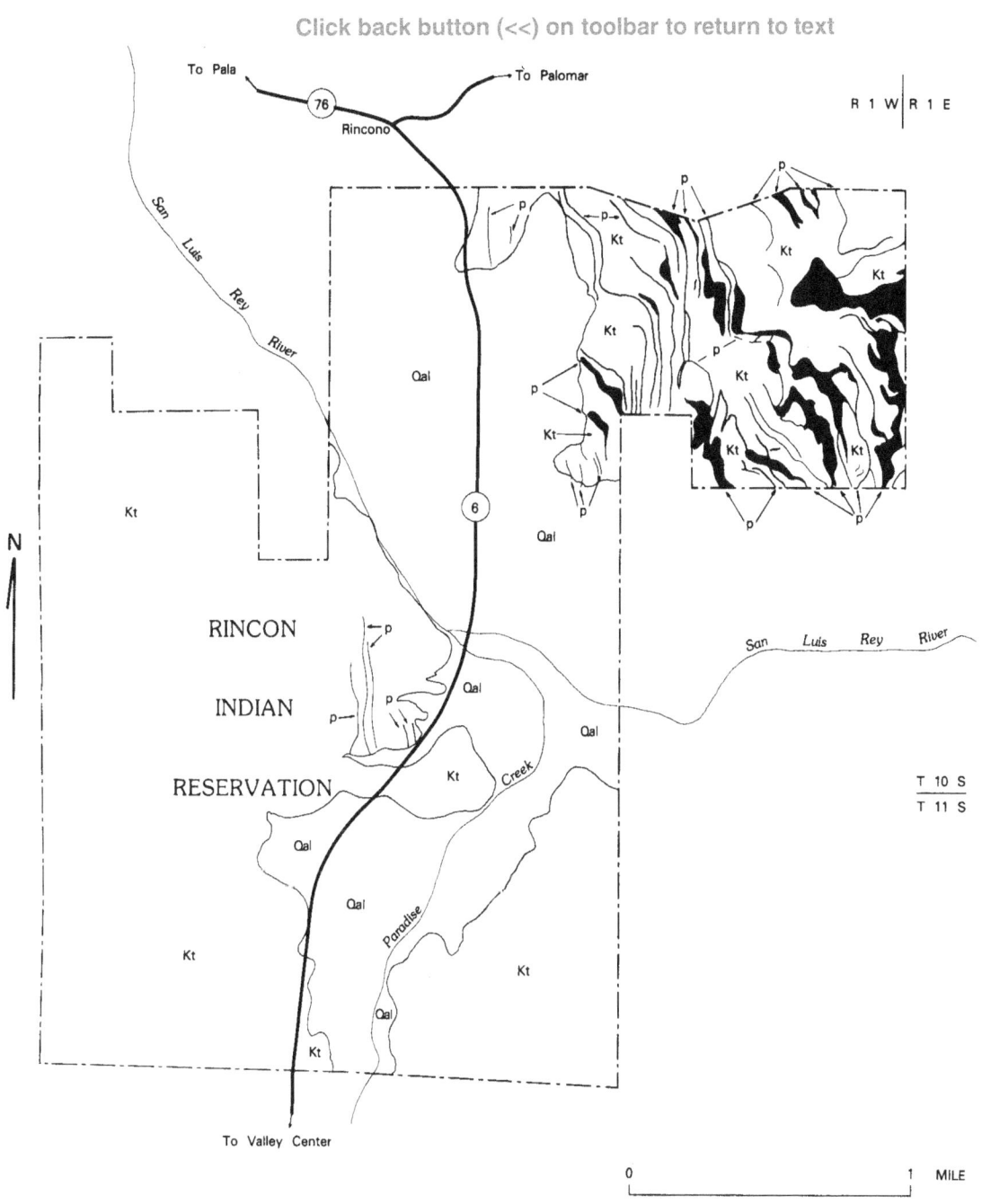

Figure 12. Geologic map of the Rincon Indian Reservation (from Hanley, 1957; Weber, 1963). Quaternary alluvium (Qal); granitic pegmatite dikes (p); tonalite (Kt).

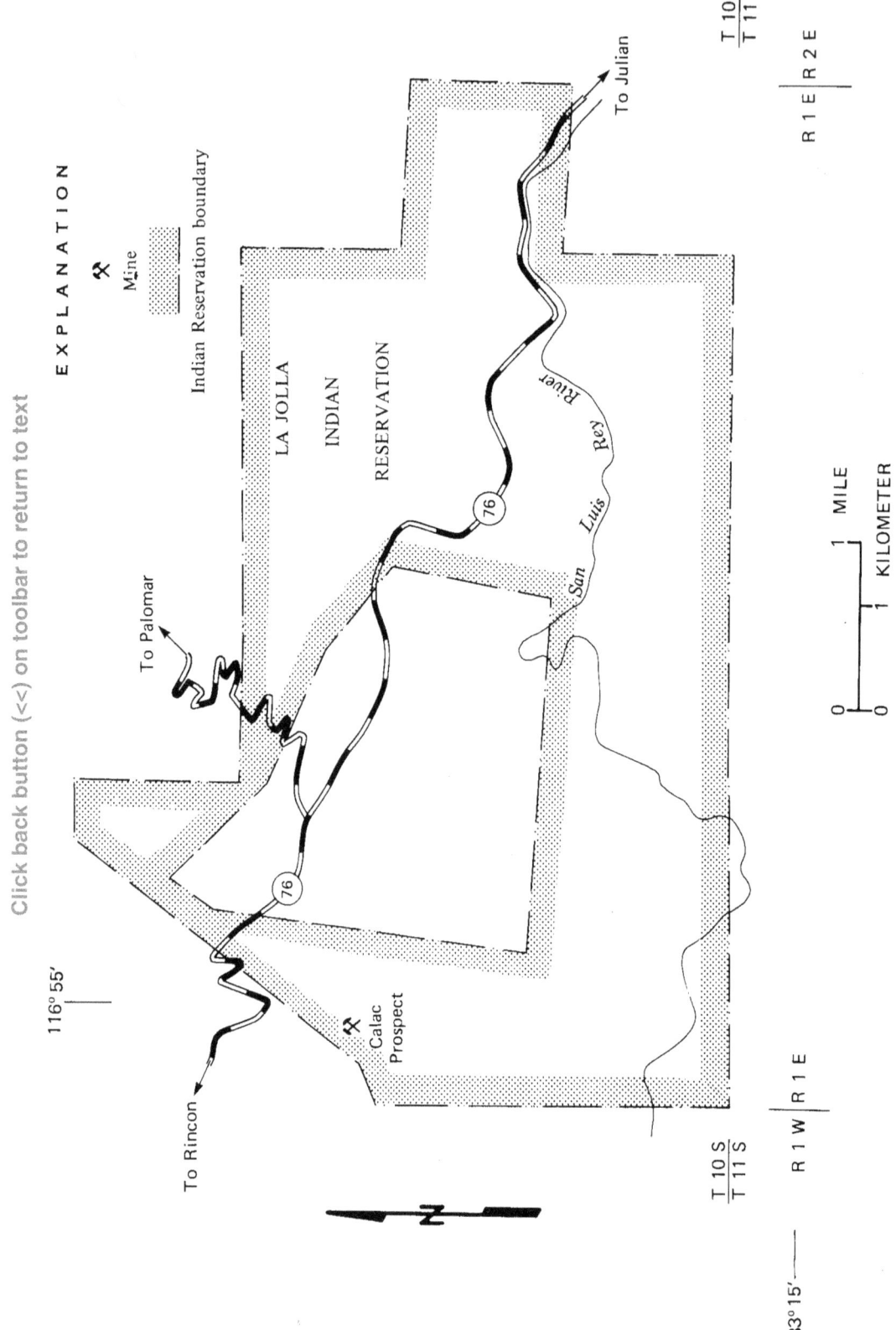

Figure 13. Mineral resource map of the La Jolla Indian Reservation.

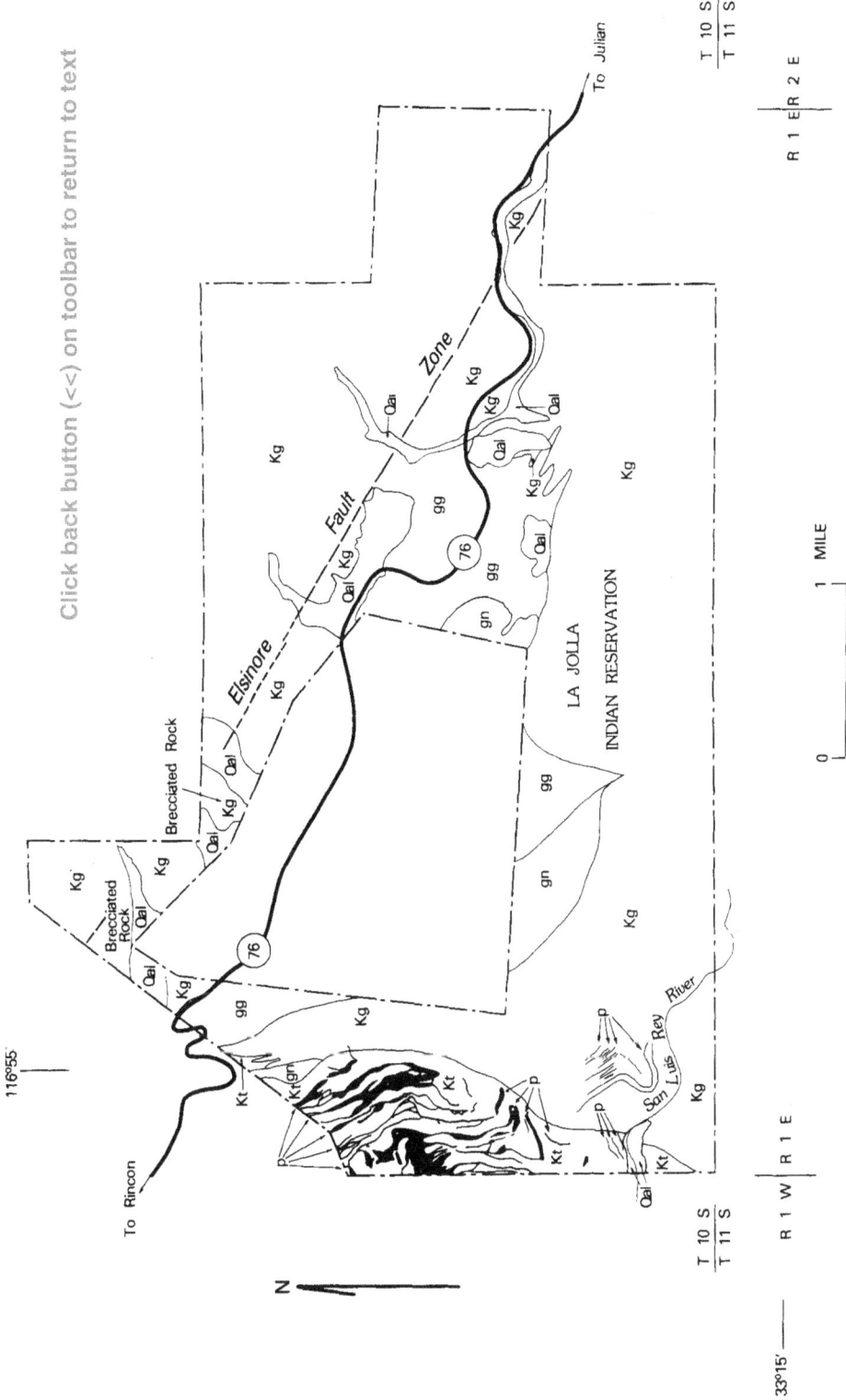

Figure 14. Geologic map of the La Jolla Indian Reservation (from Olmstead, 1953; Hanley, 1957). Quaternary alluvial deposits (Qal); granitic pegmatite dikes (p); granodiorite (Kg); tonalite (kt); gneiss and schist (gn); mixed granitic rock and gneiss (gg).

Click back button (<<) on toolbar to return to text

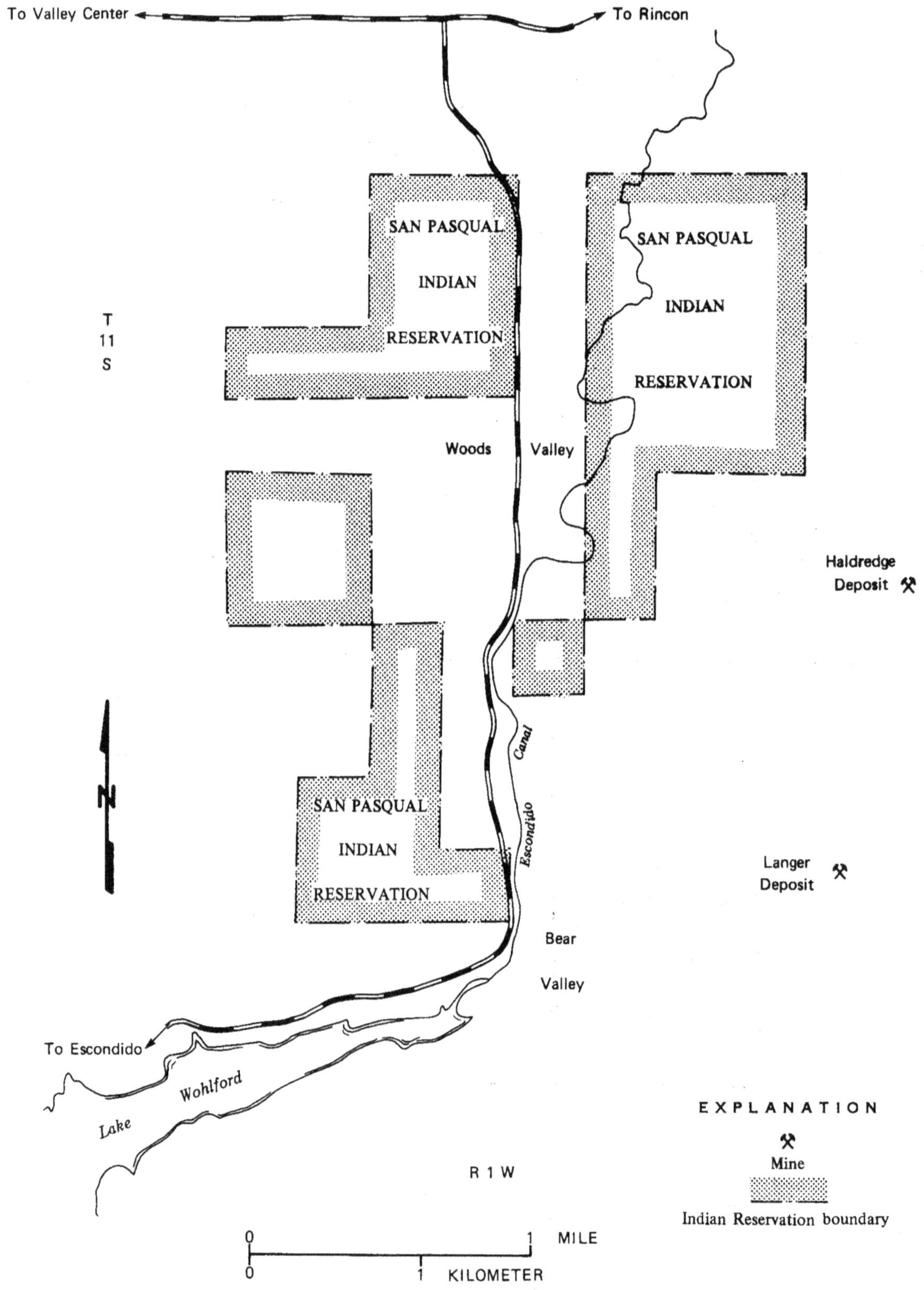

Figure 15. Mineral resource map of the San Pasqual Indian Reservation.

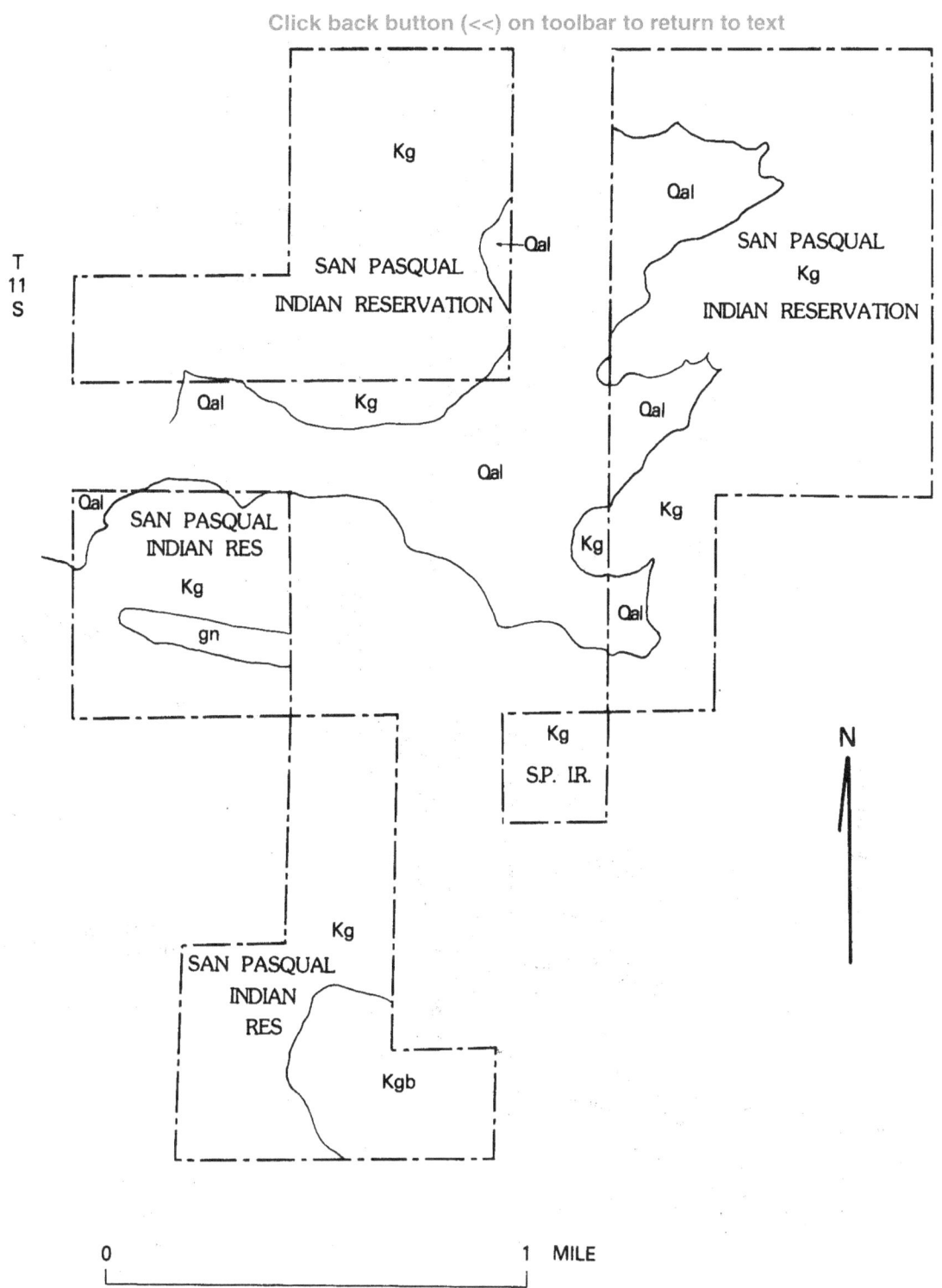

Figure 16. Geologic map of the San Pasqual Indian Reservation (from Weber, 1963). Quaternary alluvial deposits (Qal); granitic rocks (Kg); gabbro (Kgb); schist (gn).

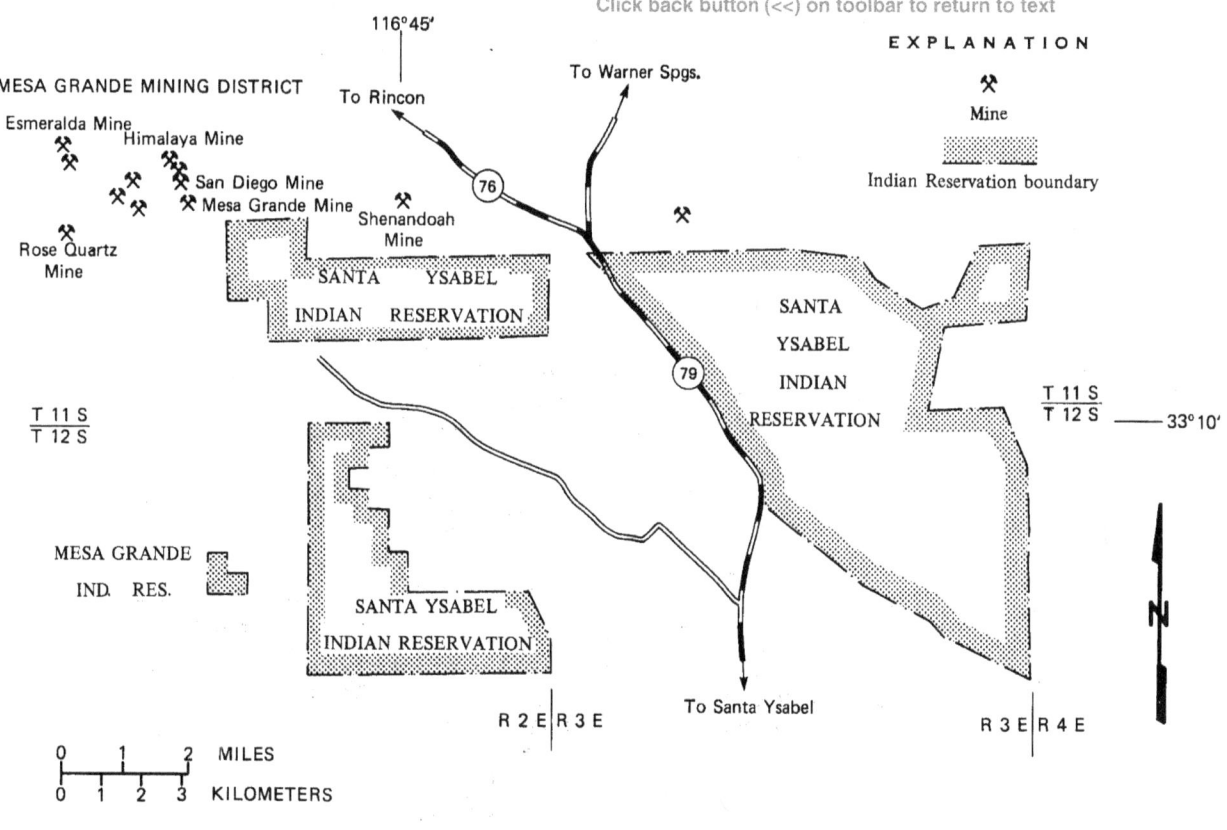

Click back button (<<) on toolbar to return to text

Figure 17. Mineral resource map of the Santa Ysabel and Mesa Grande Indian Reservations.

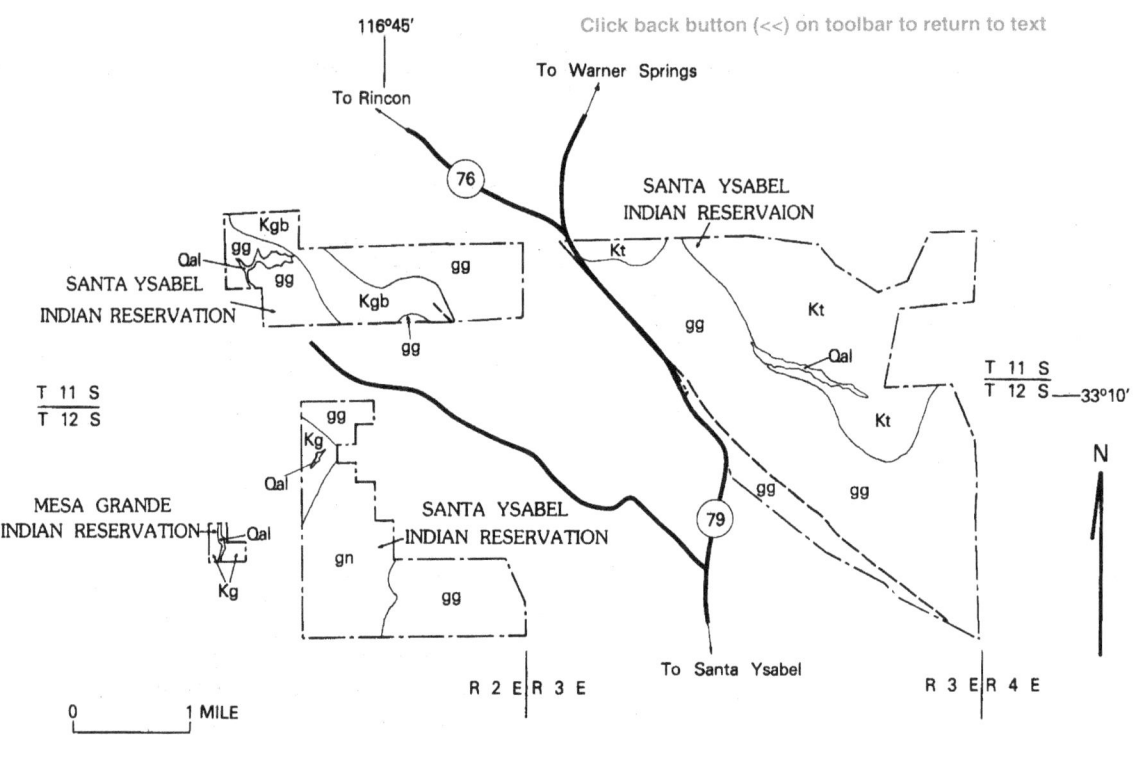

Figure 18. Geologic map of the Mesa Grande and Santa Ysabel Indian Reservations (from Merriam, 1958; Olmstead, 1953). Quaternary alluvium (Qal); granodiorite (Kg); tonalite (Kt); gabbro (Kgb); schist and gneiss (gn); mixed gneiss and granitic rock (gg).

Click back button (<<) on toolbar to return to text

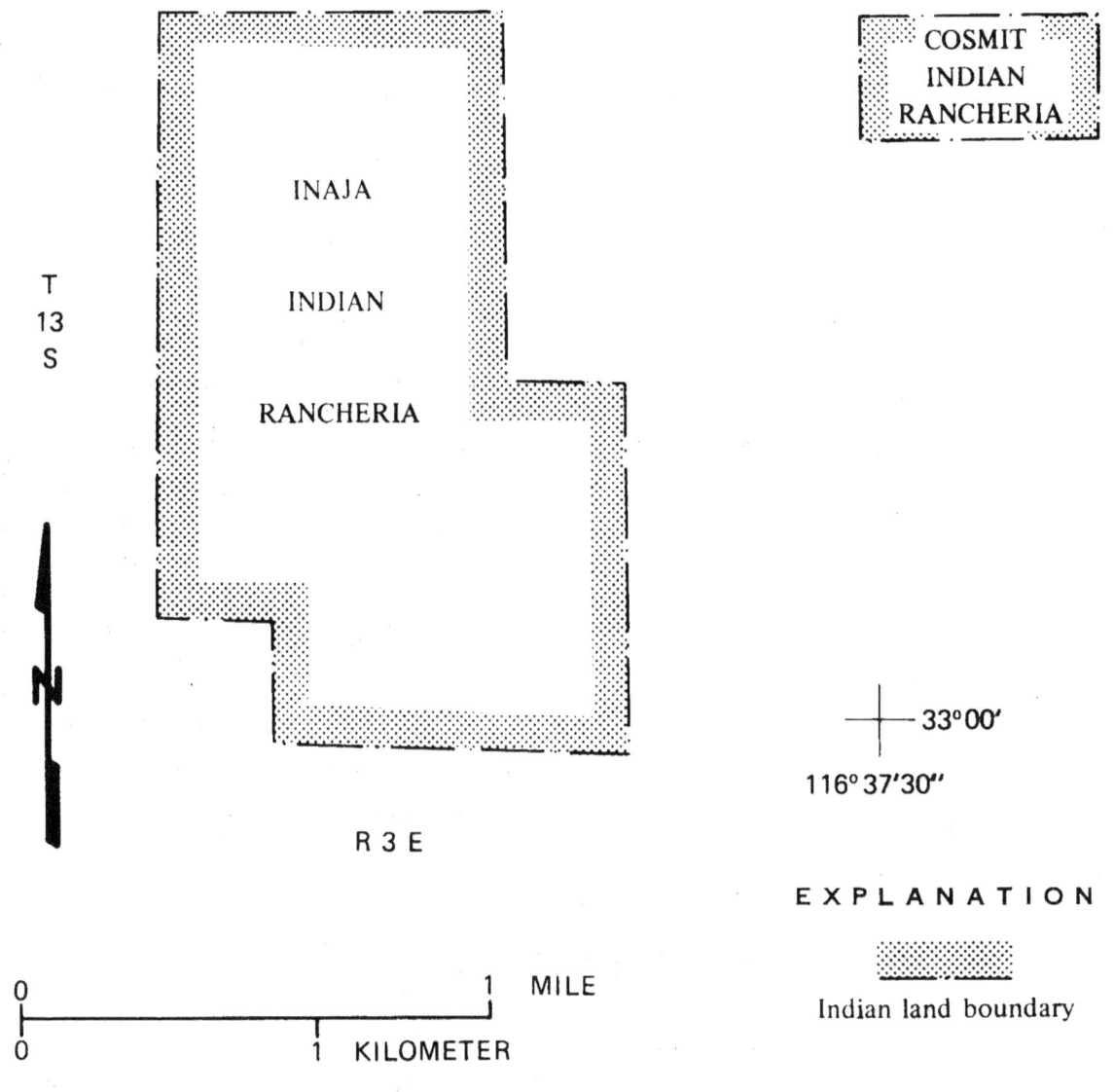

Figure 19. Mineral resource map of the Inaja-Cosmit Indian Rancheria.

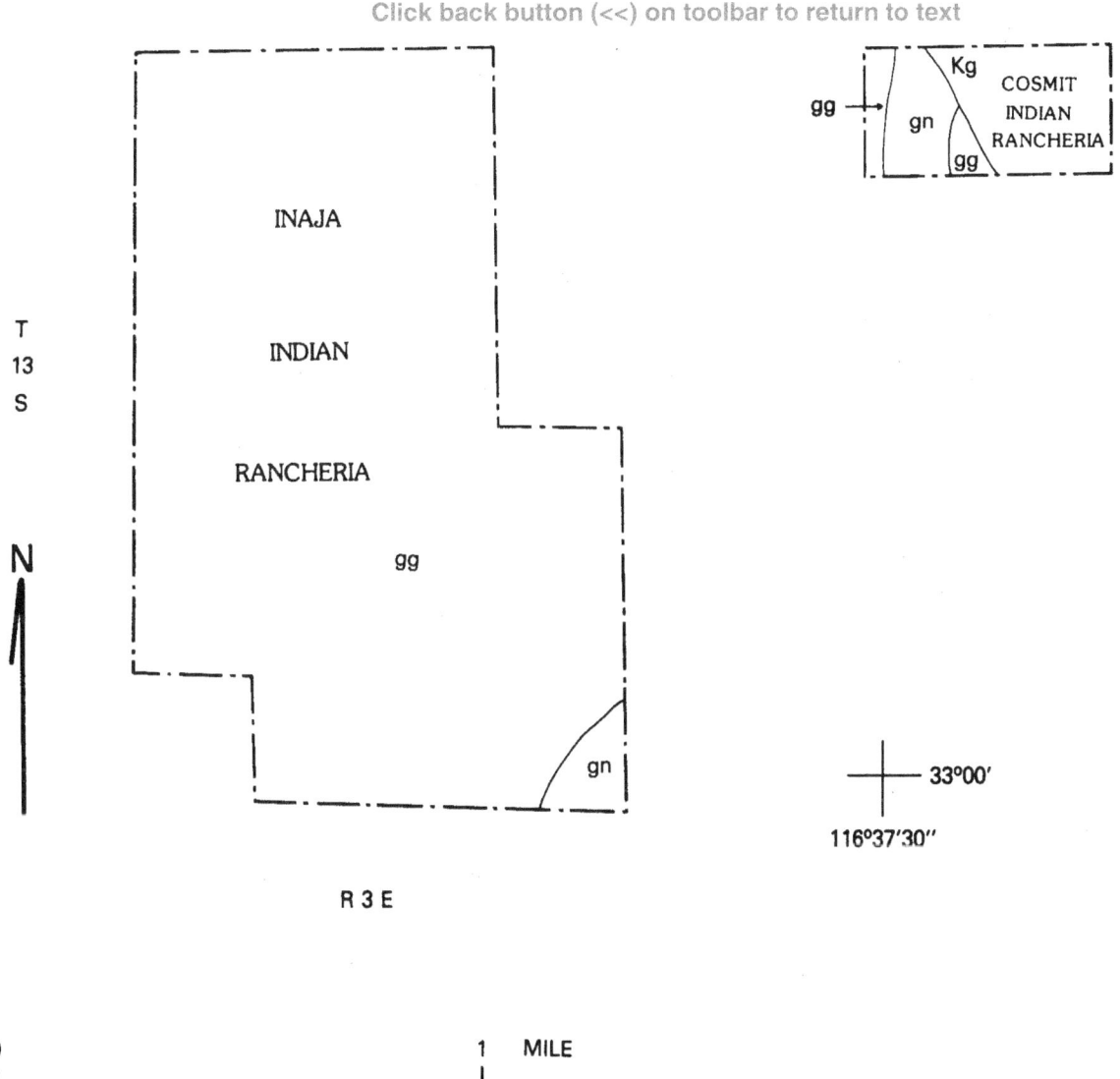

Figure 20. Geologic map of the Inaja Indian Rancheria and the Cosmit Indian Rancheria (from Merriam, 1958). Gabbro (Kg); mixed gneiss and granitic rock (gg); gneiss and schist (gn).

Click back button (<<) on toolbar to return to text

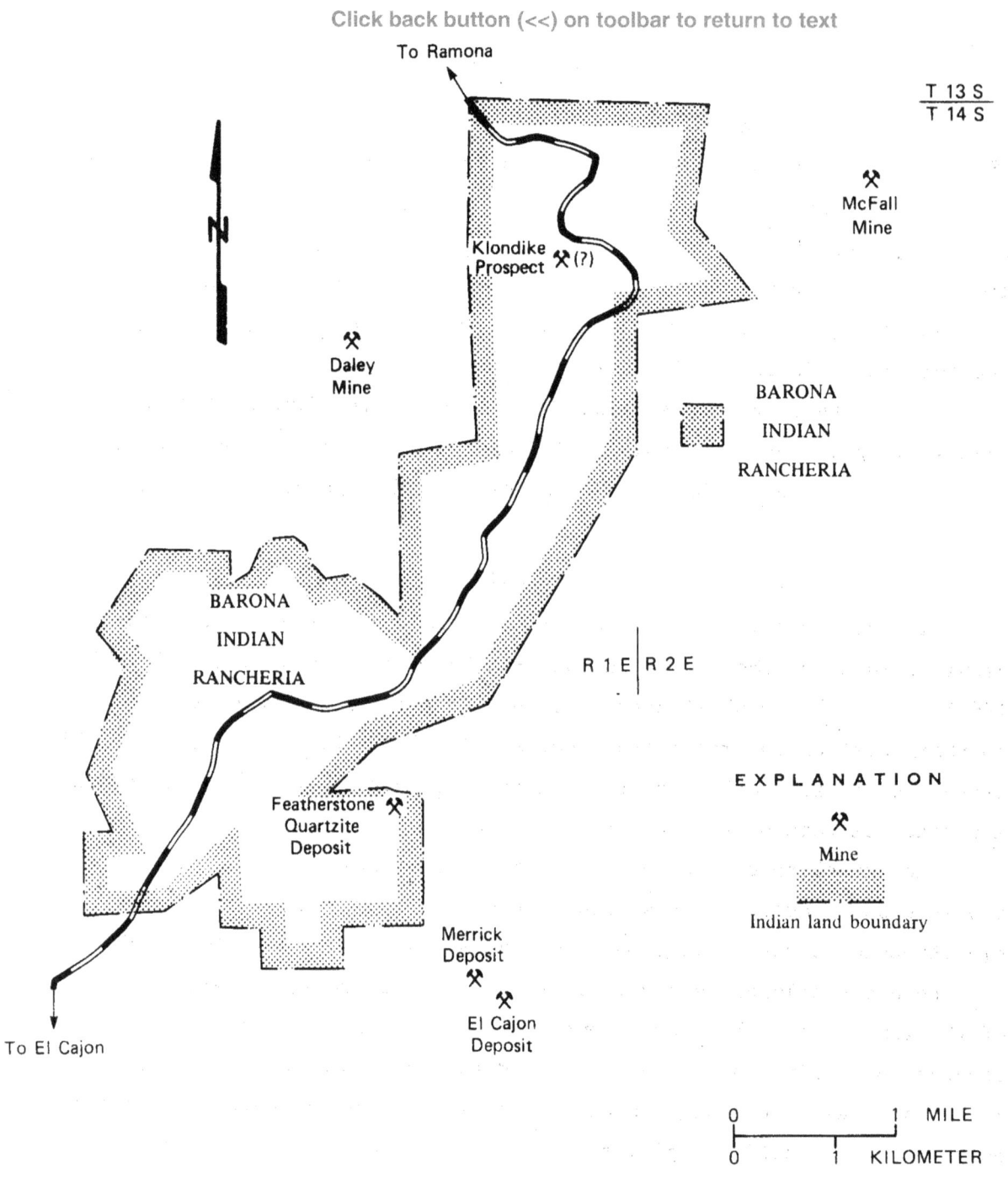

Figure 21. Mineral resource map of the Barona Indian Rancheria.

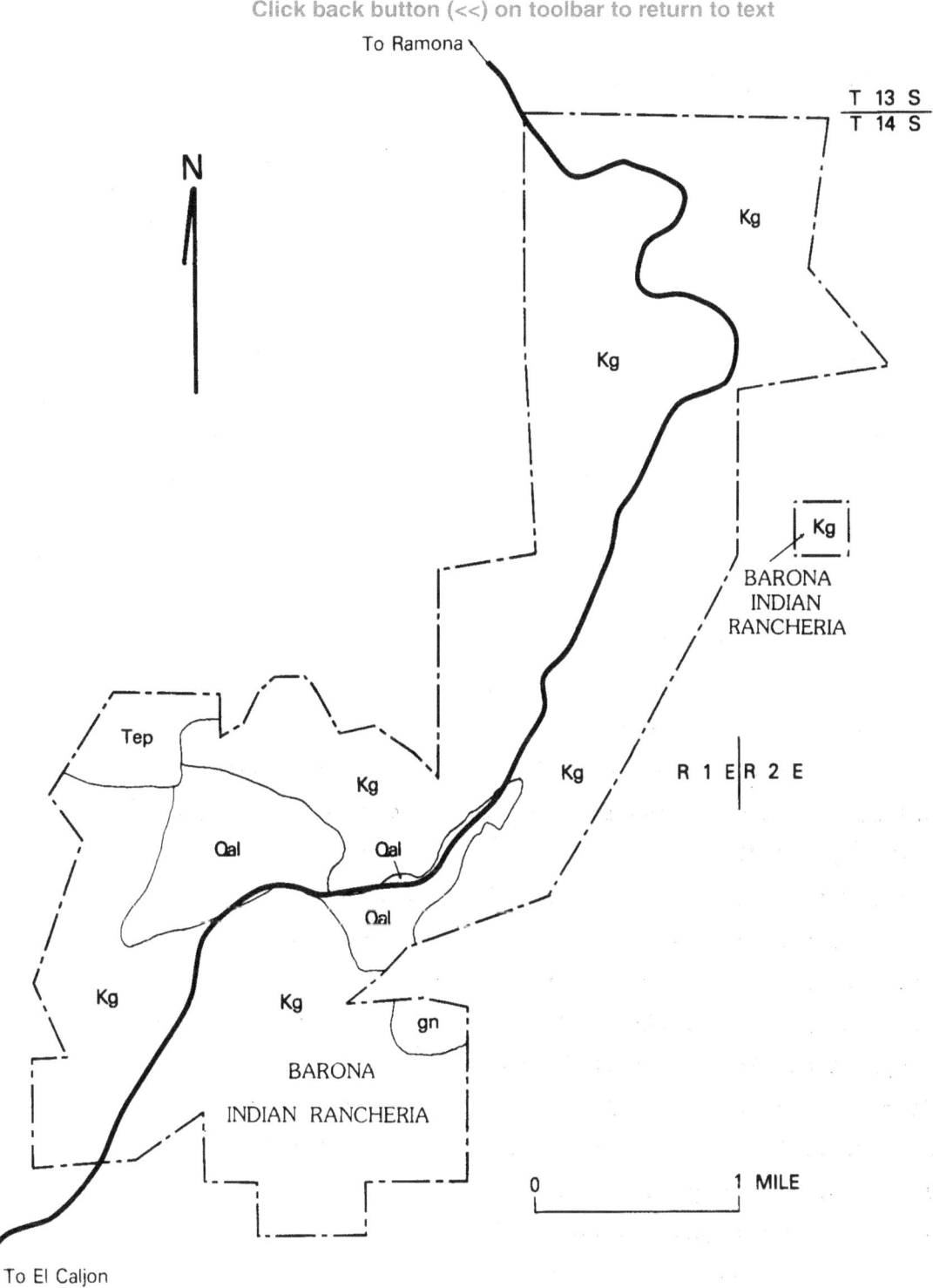

Figure 22. Geologic map of the Barona Indian Rancheria (from Weber, 1963). Quaternary alluvium (Qal); Poway Conglomerate (Tep); granitic rocks, undivided (Kg); schist and gneiss (gn).

Click back button (<<) on toolbar to return to text

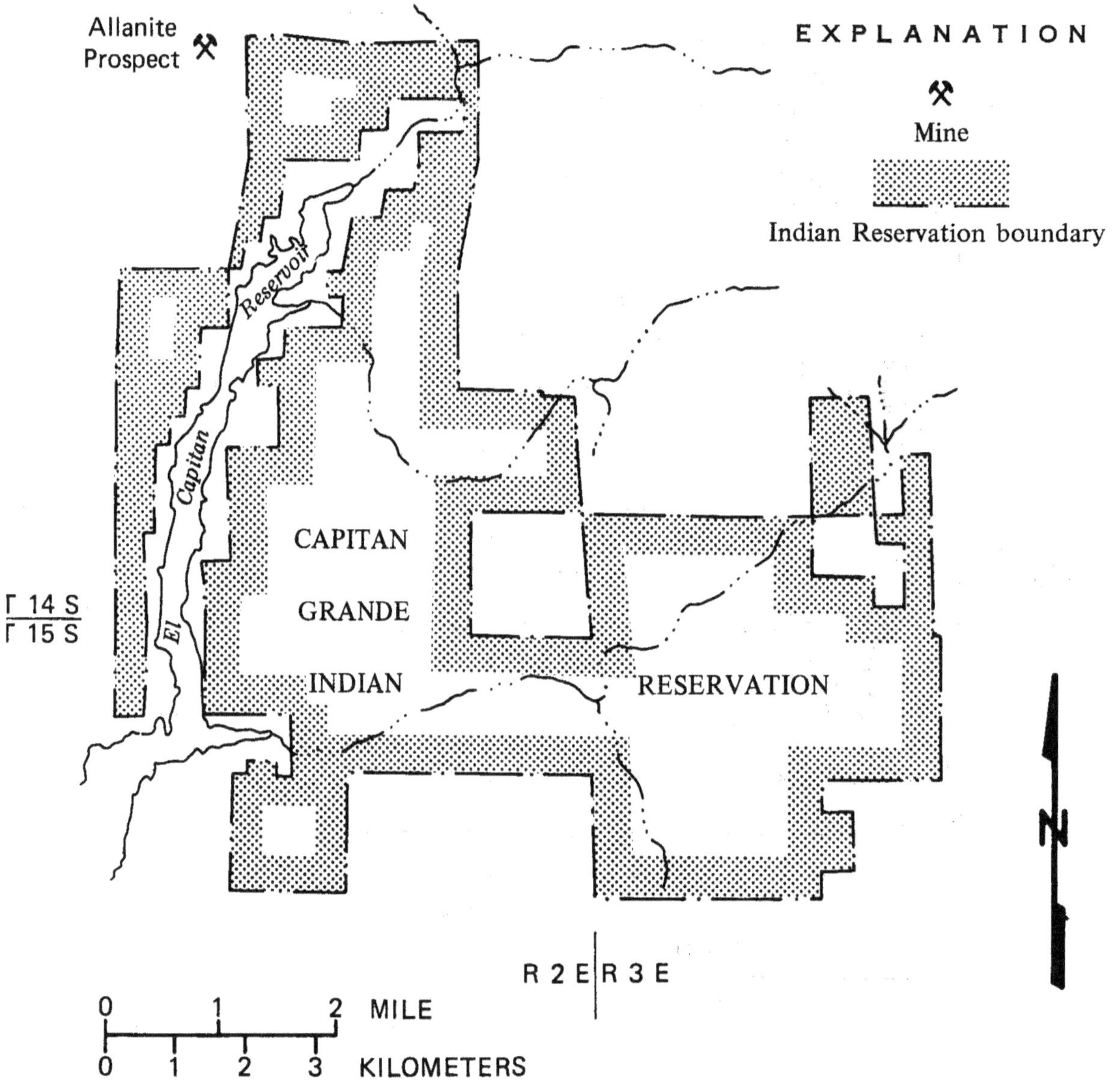

Allanite Prospect ⚒

EXPLANATION

⚒
Mine

Indian Reservation boundary

Reservoir

El Capitan

CAPITAN

GRANDE

INDIAN

RESERVATION

Γ 14 S
Γ 15 S

R 2 E | R 3 E

N

0   1   2   MILE
0   1   2   3   KILOMETERS

Figure 23. Mineral resource map of the Capitan Grande Indian Reservation.

Click back button (<<) on toolbar to return to text

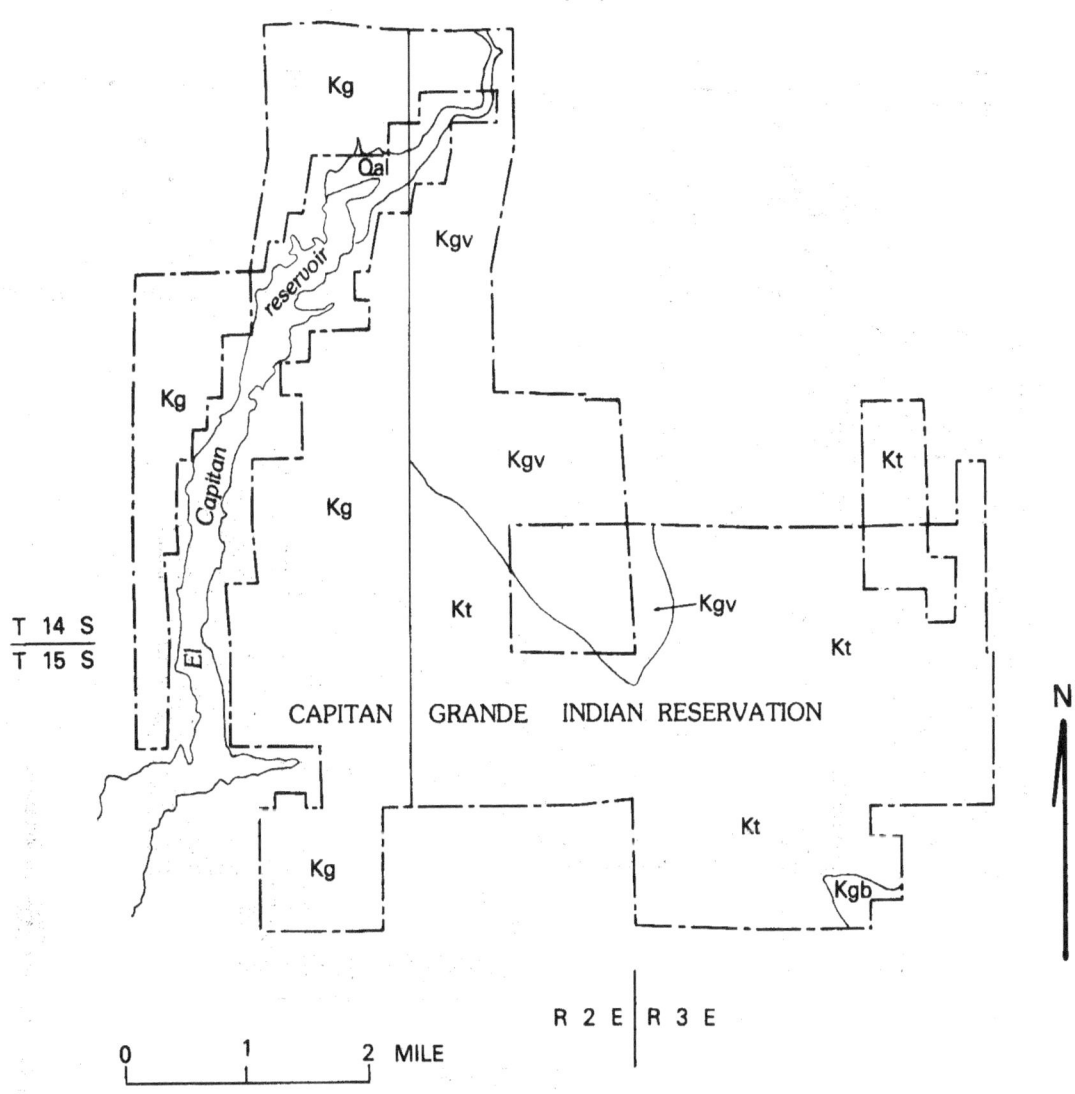

Figure 24. Geologic map of the Capitan Grande Indian Reservation (from Everhart, 1951; Weber, 1963). Undifferentiated granitic rock west of 116°45' (Kg); Bonsall tonalite (Kt); Green Valley tonalite (Kgr); gabbro (Kgb).

Click back button (<<) on toolbar to return to text

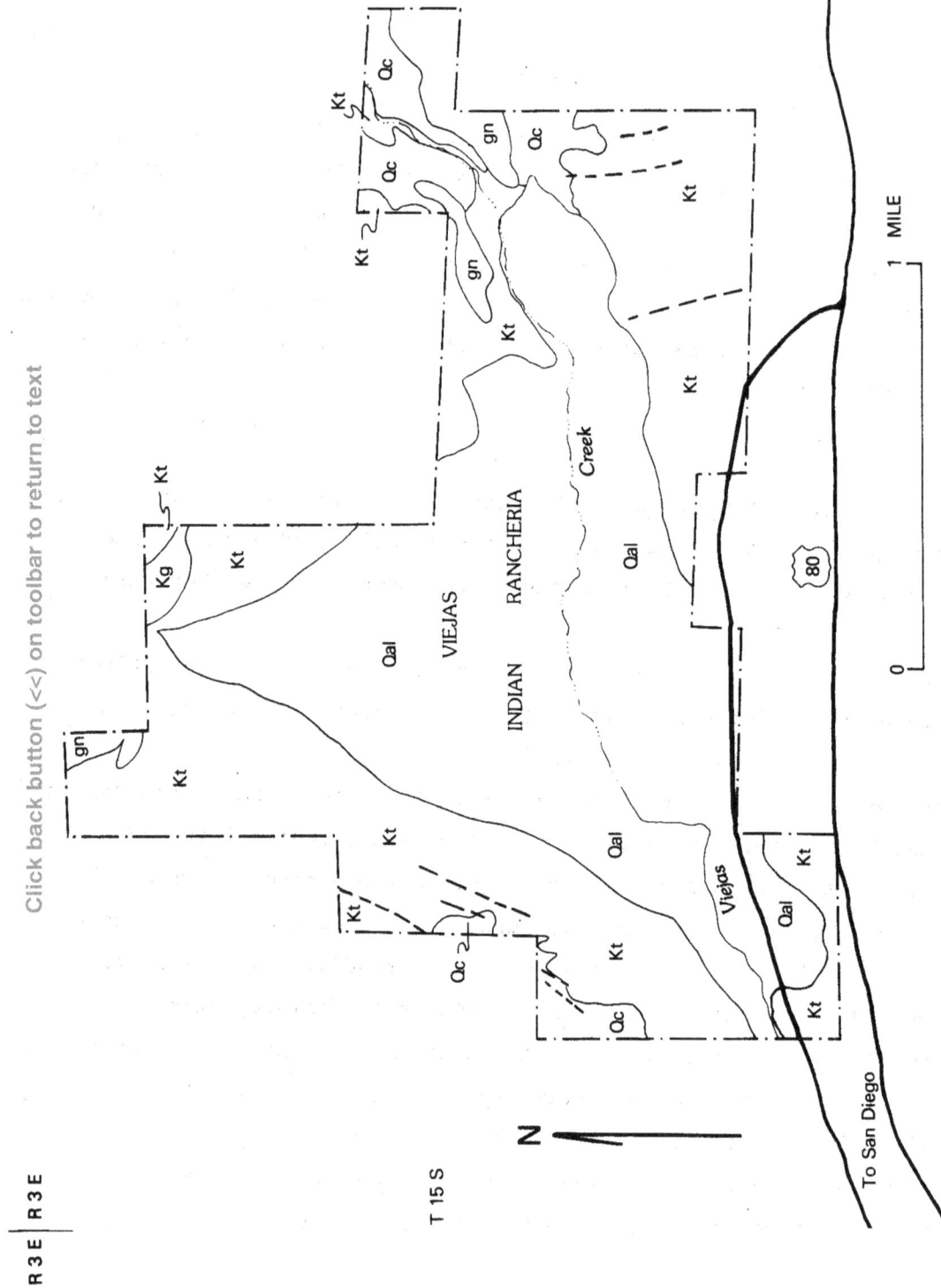

Figure 25. Geologic map of the Viejas Indian Rancheria (from Todd, 1978). Quaternary alluvium (Qal); Quaternary colluvium (Qc); tonalite (kt); gabbro (Kg); schist (gn).

Click back button (<<) on toolbar to return to text

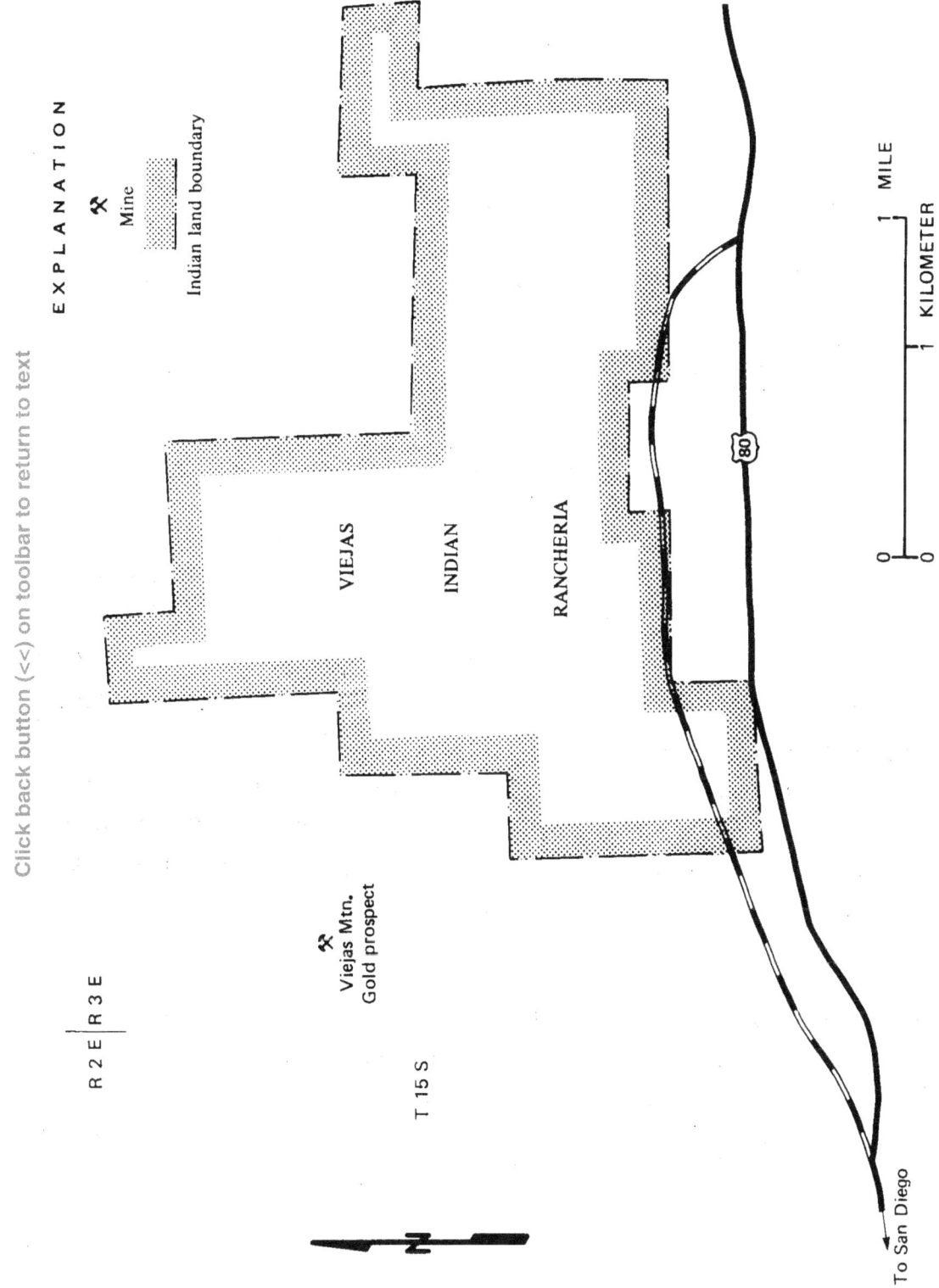

Figure 26. Mineral resource map of the Viejas Indian Rancheria.

Click back button (<<) on toolbar to return to text

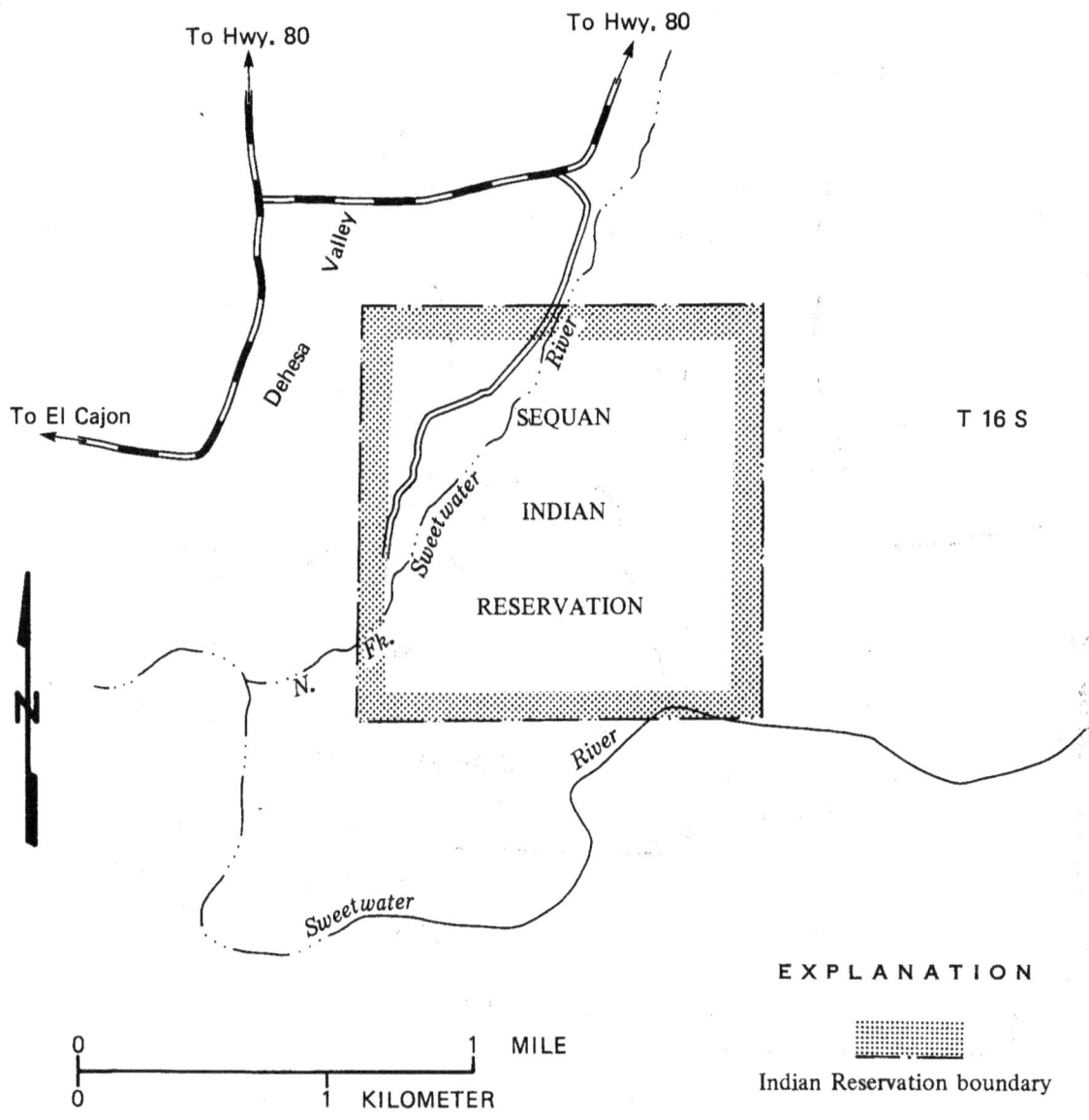

Figure 27. Mineral resource map of the Sycuan Indian Reservation.

Click back button (<<) on toolbar to return to text

R 1 E | R 2 E

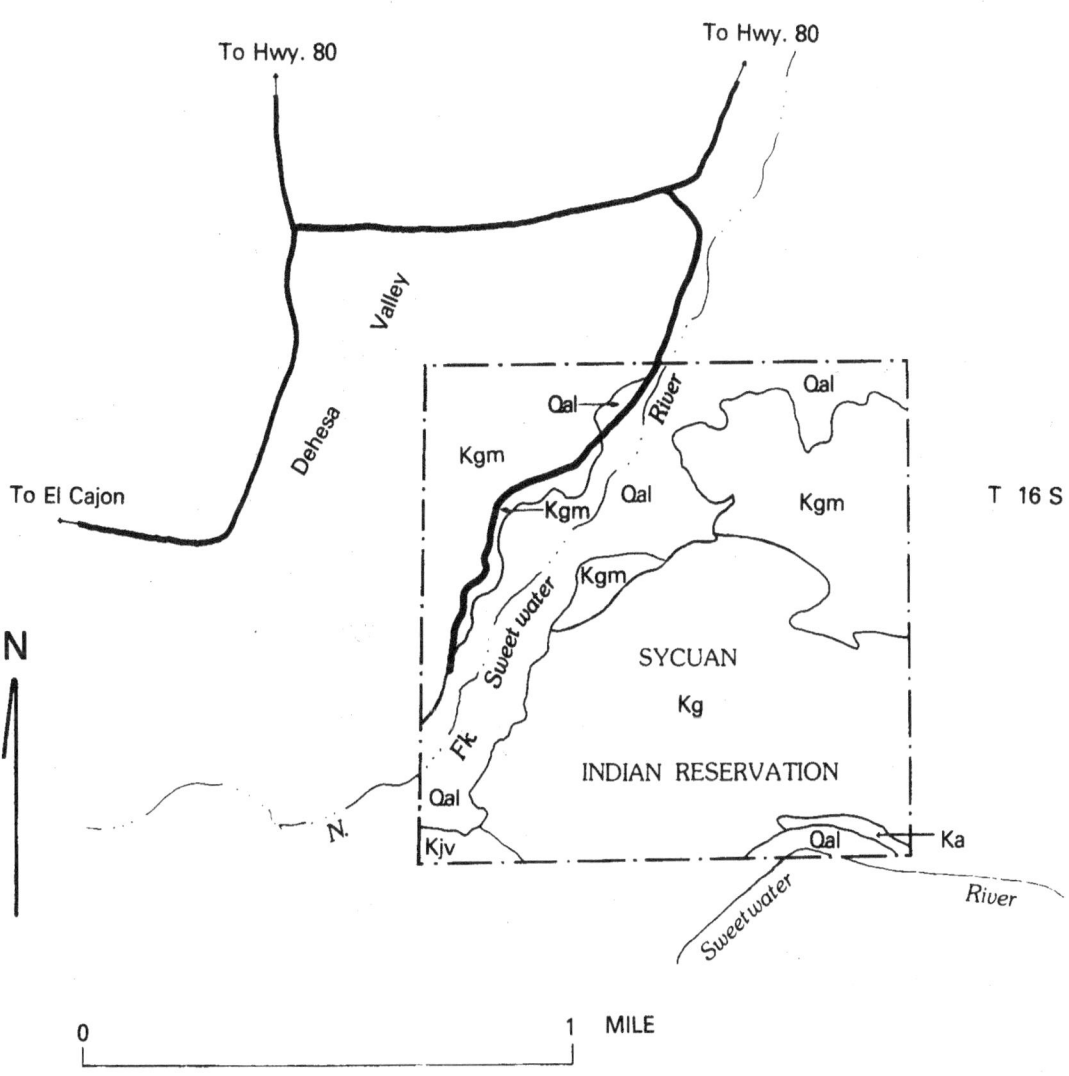

Figure 28. Geologic map of the Sycuan (Sequan) Indian Reservation (from Todd, 1980). Quaternary alluvium (Qal); tonalite of Granite Mountain (Kgm); tonalite of Japatul Valley (Kjr); tonalite of Alpine (Ka); gabbro (Kg).

Click back button (<<) on toolbar to return to text

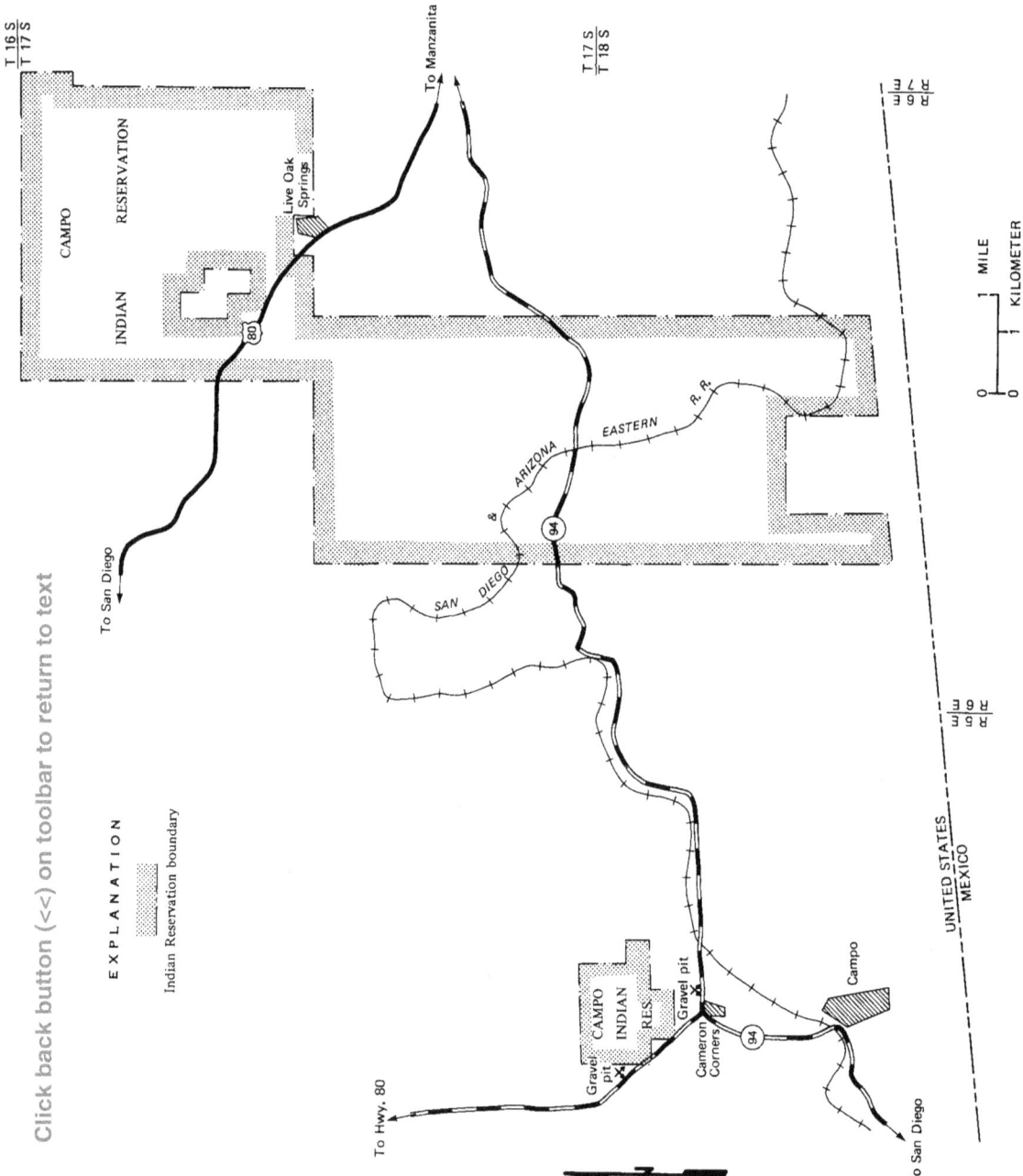

Figure 29. Mineral resource map of the Campo Indian Reservation.

Click back button (<<) on toolbar to return to text

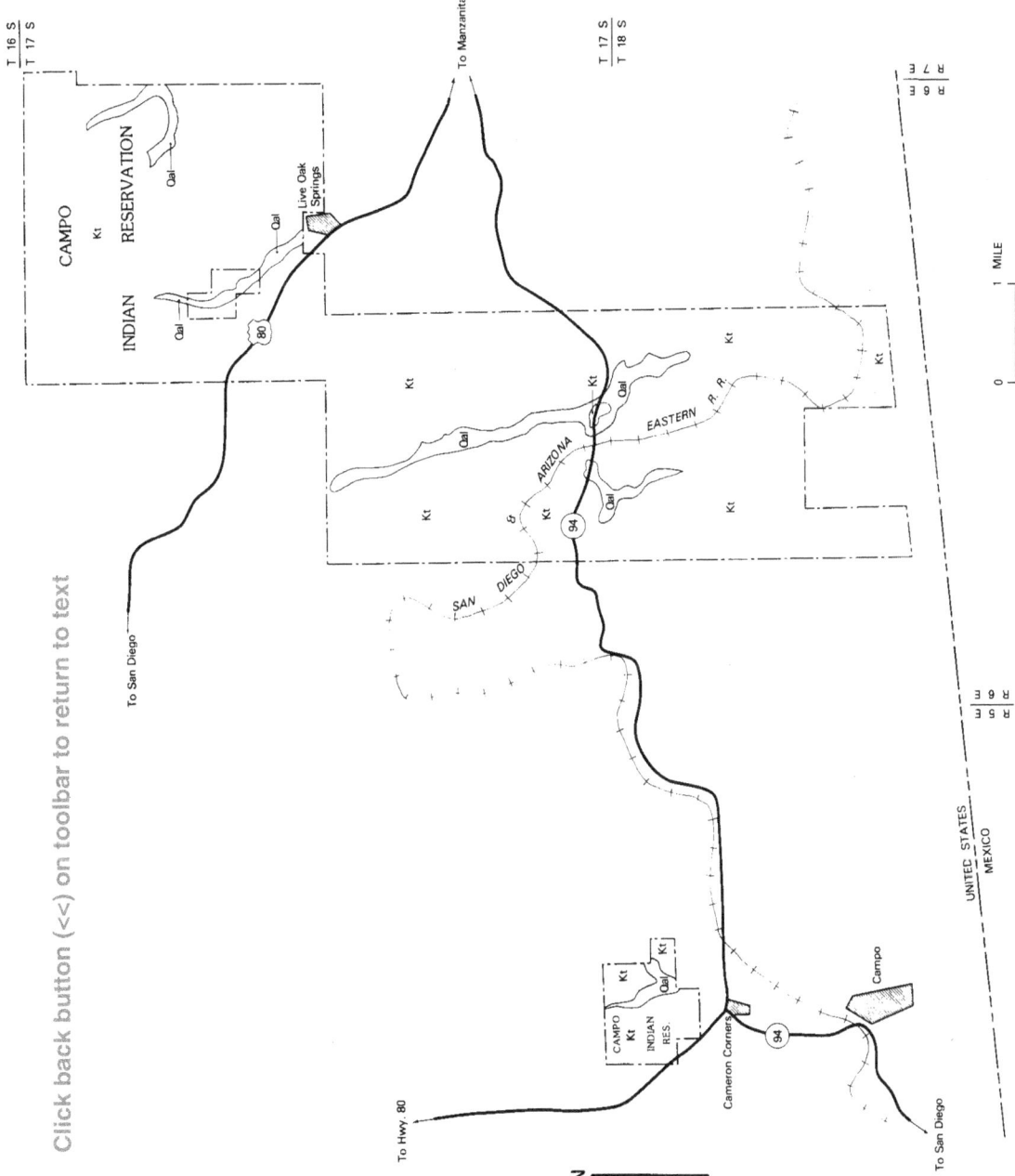

Figure 30. Geologic map of the Campo Indian Reservation (from Olmstead, 1953). Quaternary alluvium (Qal); tonalite (Kt).

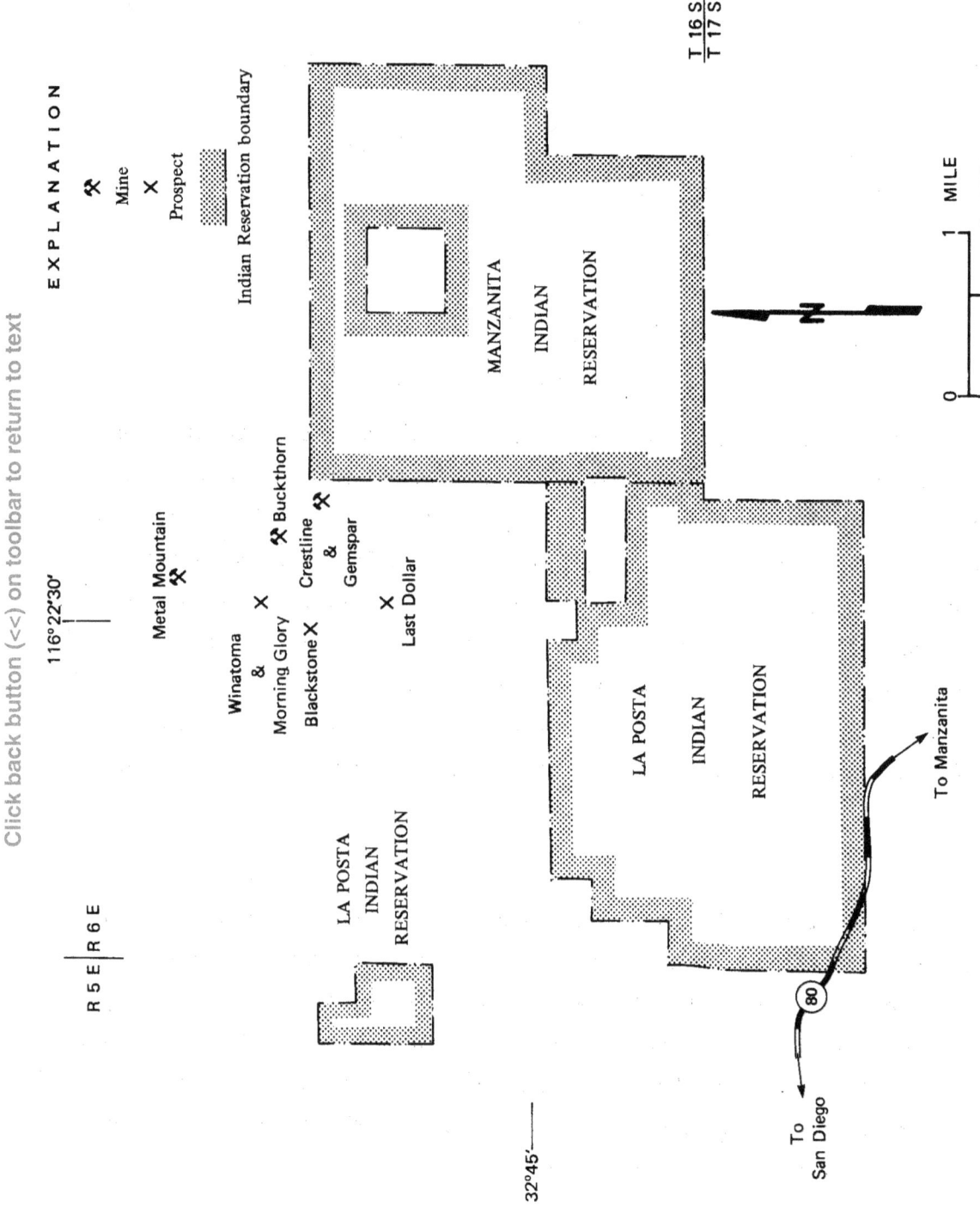

Figure 31. Mineral resource map of the La Posta and Manzanita Indian Reservations.

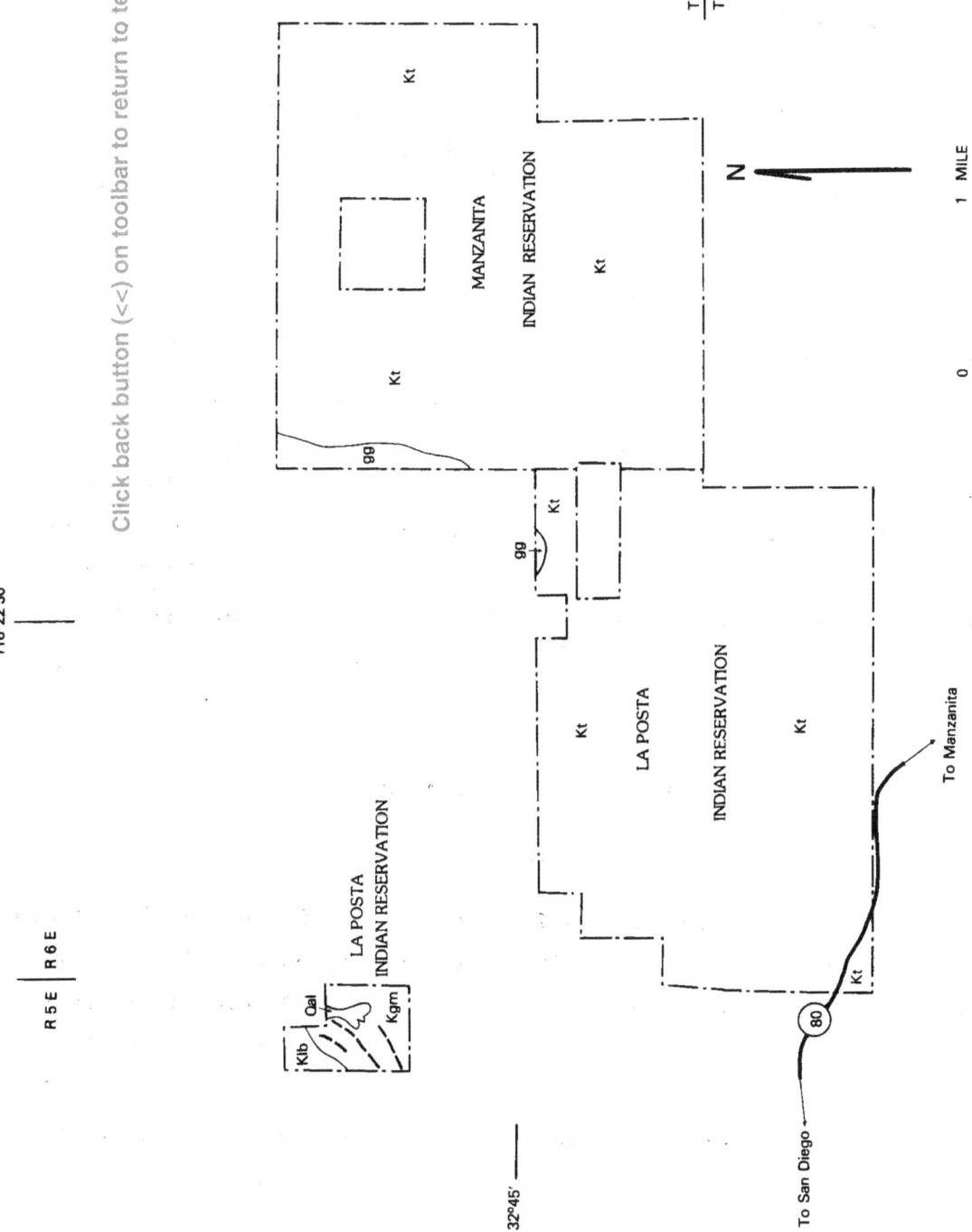

Figure 32. Geologic map of the La Posta and Manzanita Indian Reservations, (from Weber, 1963; Todd, 1979). Quaternary alluvial deposits (Qal); tonalite (Kt); tonalite of Las Bancas (Klb); tonalite of Granite Mountain (Kgm); mixed granitic rock and schist (gg).

Click back button (<<) on toolbar to return to text

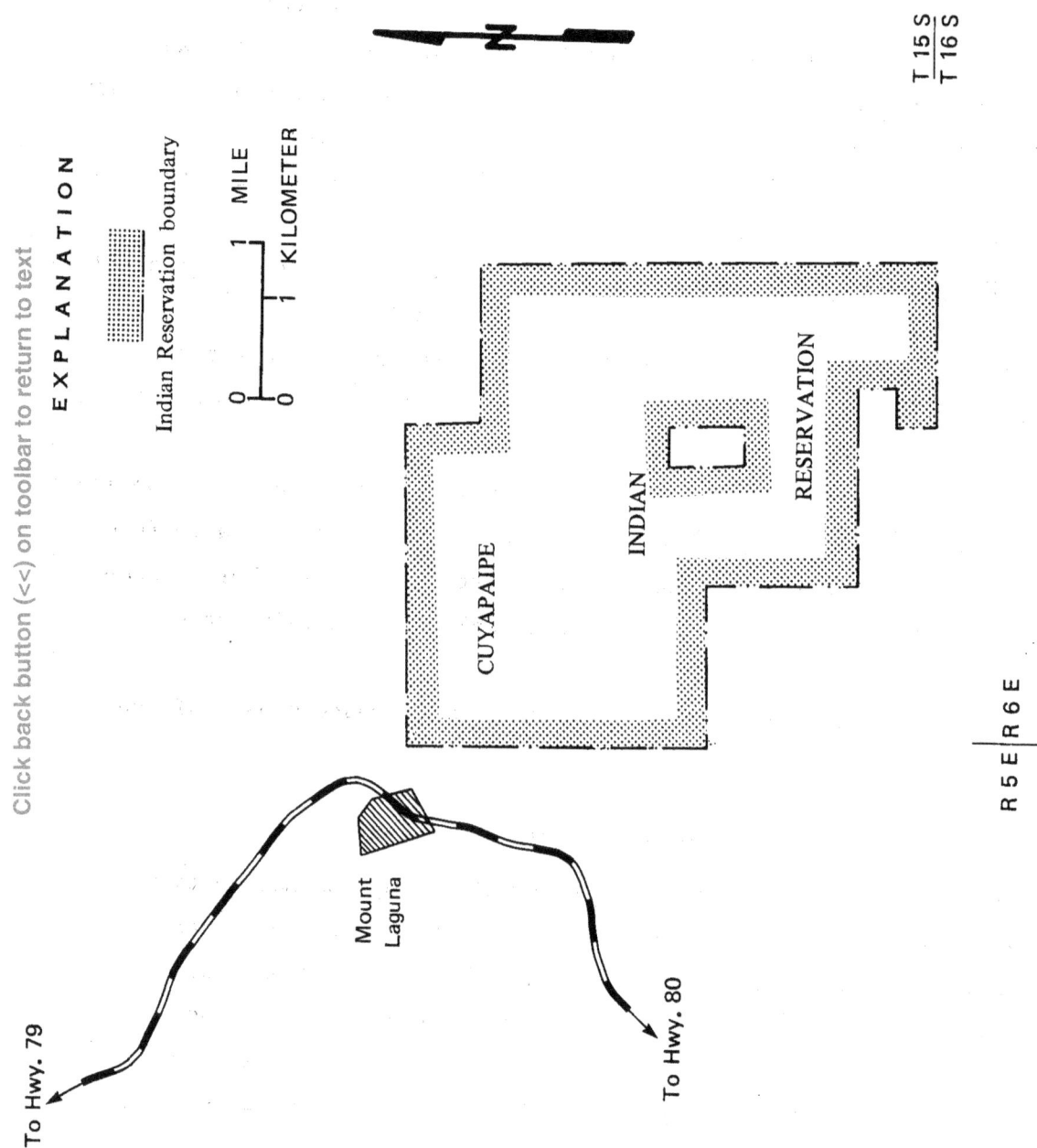

Figure 33. Mineral resource map of the Cuyapaipe Indian Reservation.

Click back button (<<) on toolbar to return to text

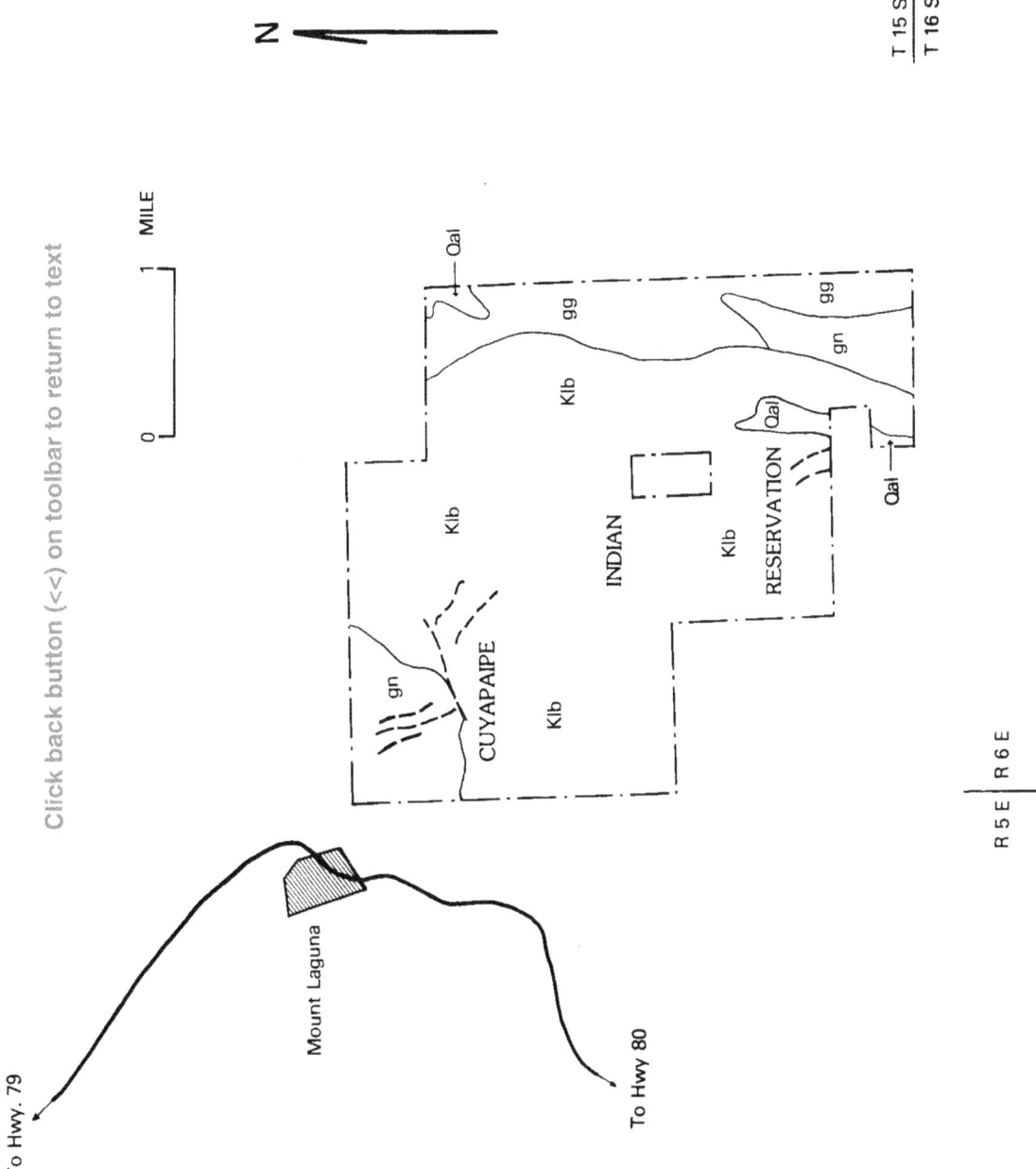

Figure 34. Geologic map of the Cuyapaipe Indian Reservation (from Todd, 1978; Weber, 1963). Quaternary alluvium (Qal); tonalite of Las Bancas (Klb); granitic rock, undifferentiated (Kg); schist and gneiss (gn); mixed granitic rock and schist (gg).

Click back button (<<) on toolbar to return to text

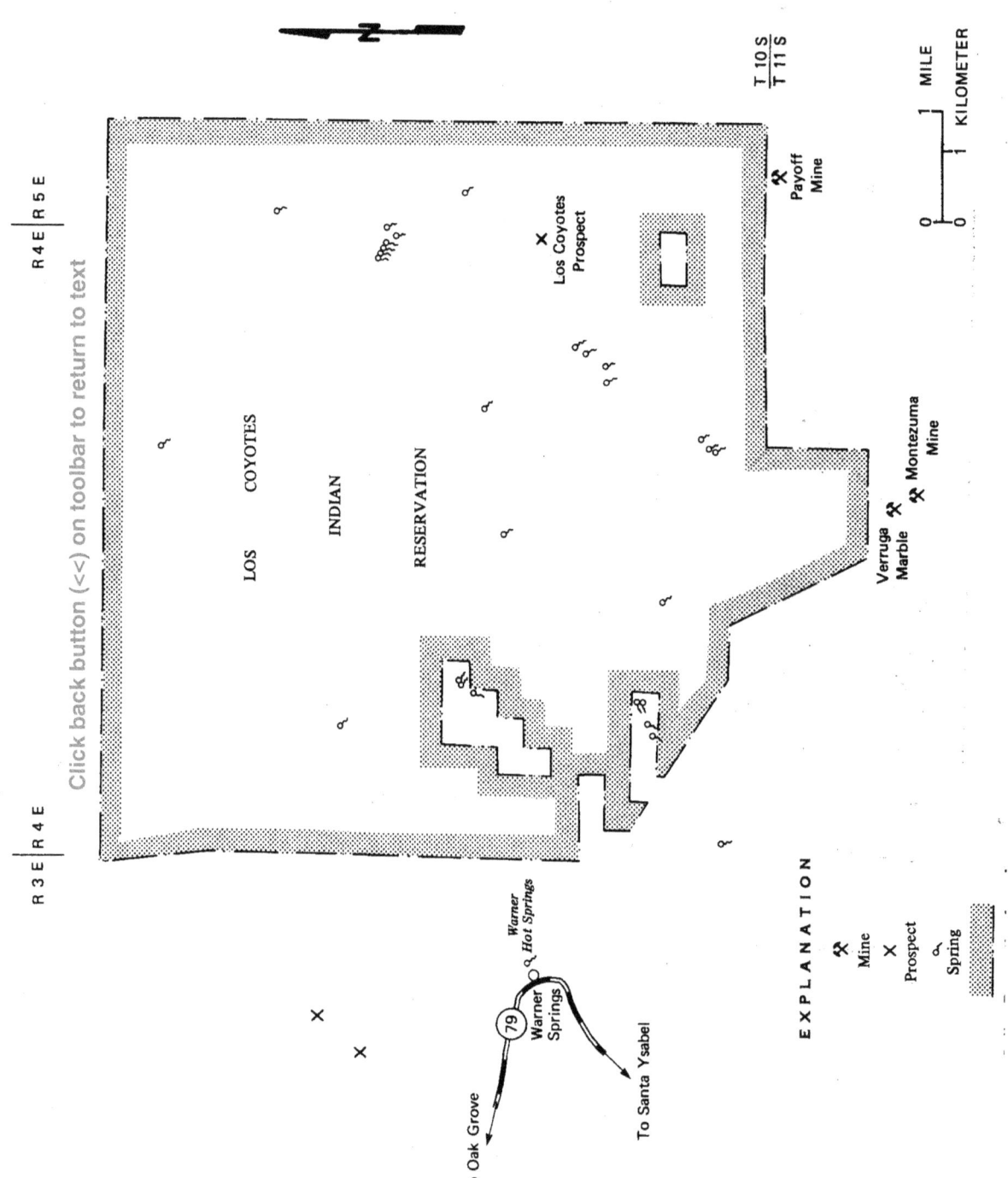

Figure 35. Mineral resource map of the Los Coyotes Indian Reservation.

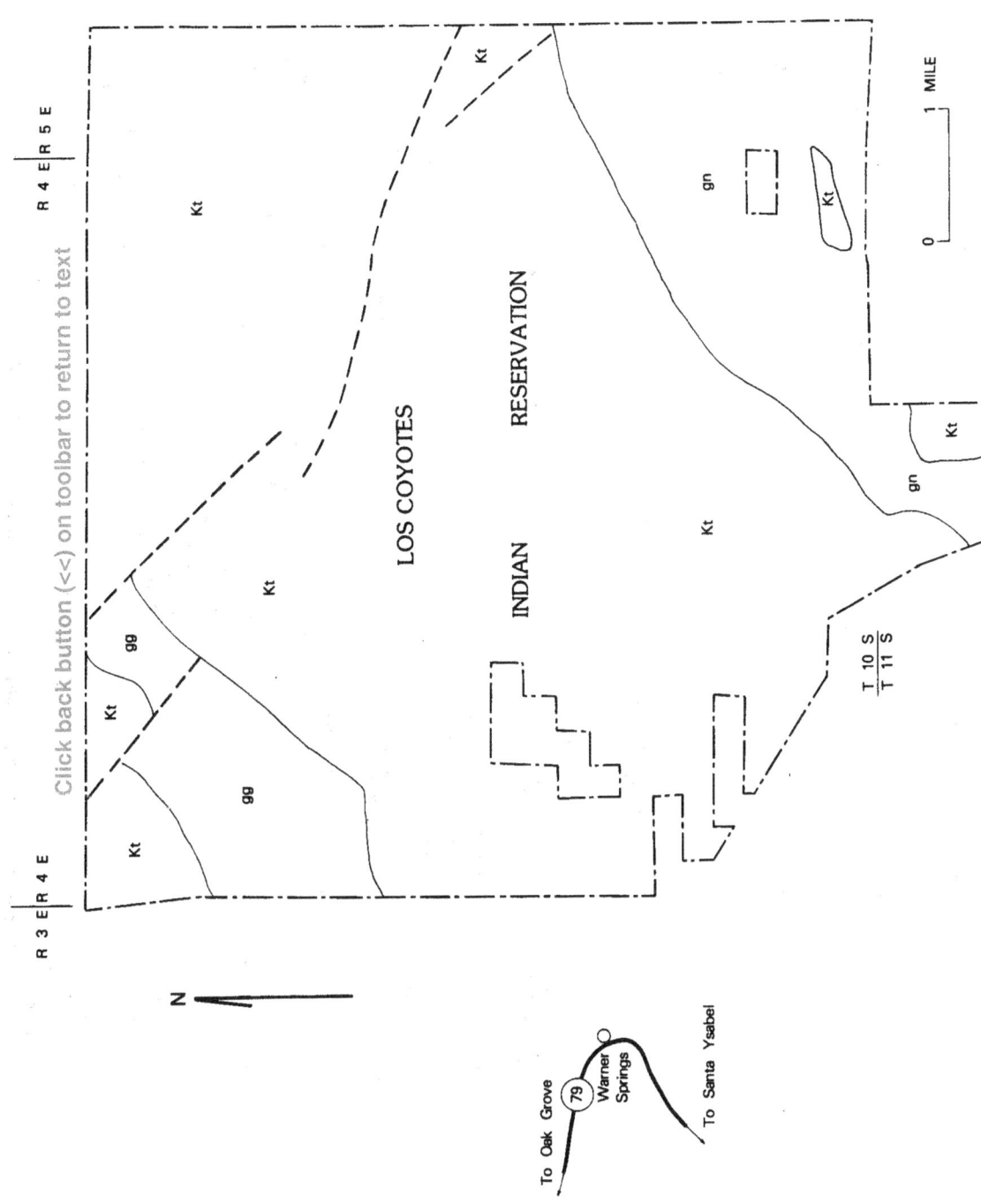

Click back button (<<) on toolbar to return to text

Figure 36. Geologic map of the Los Coyotes Indian Reservation (from Weber, 1963). Tonalite and granodiorite (Kt); schist and gneiss (gn); mixed granitic rocks and schist (gg).

Click back button (<<) on toolbar to return to text

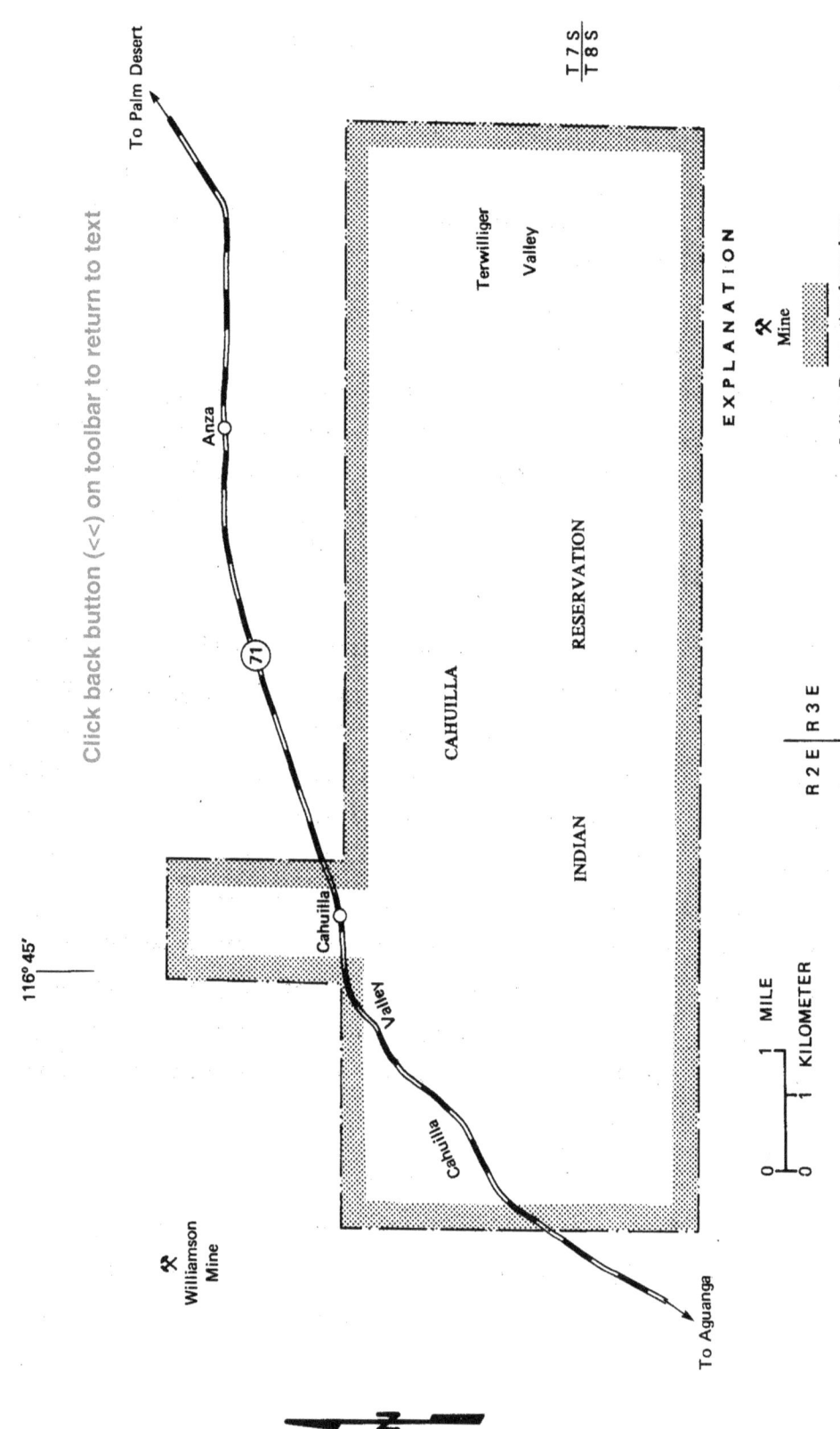

Figure 37. Mineral resource map of the Cahuilla Indian Reservation.

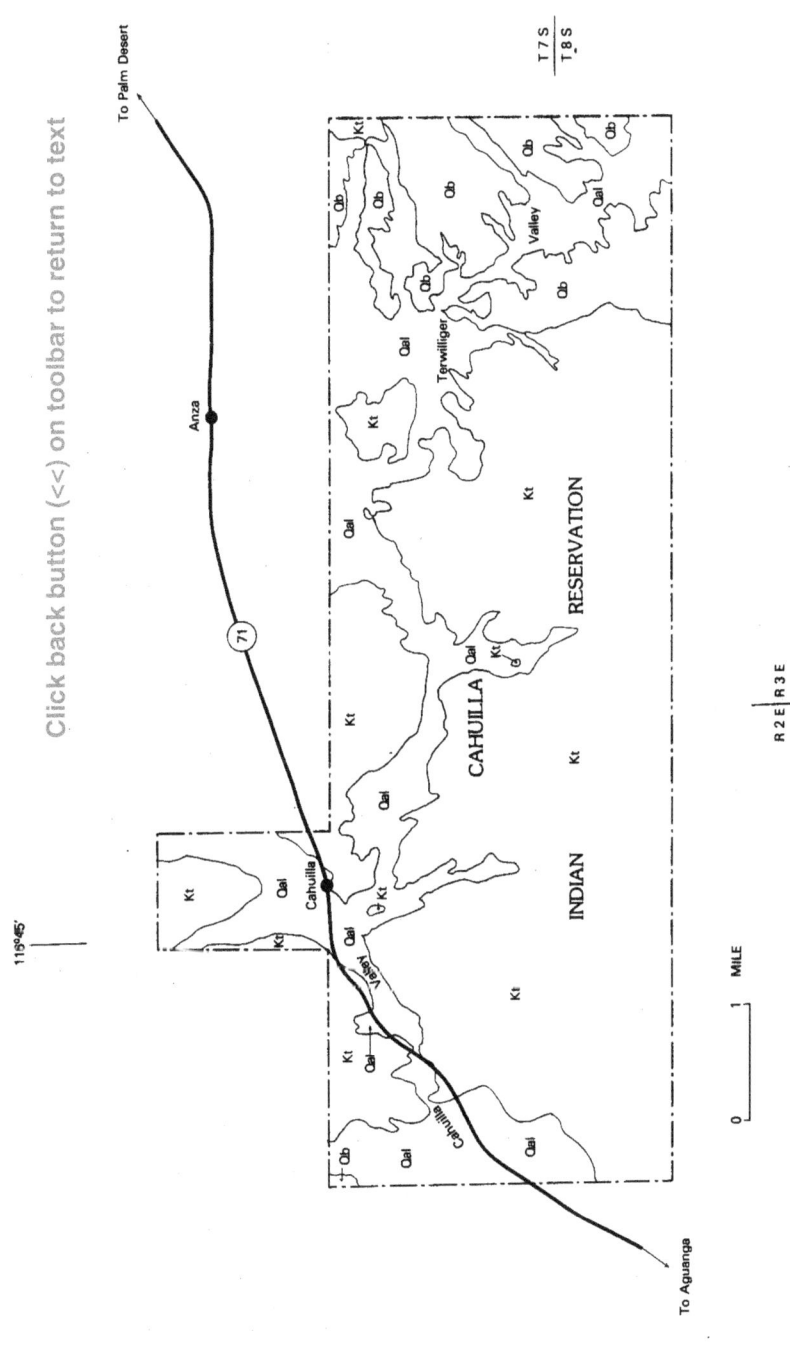

Figure 38. Geologic map of the Cahuilla Indian Reservation (from Sharp, 1967; Rogers, 1965). Quaternary alluvial deposits (Qal); Bautista beds (Qb); tonalite (Kt).

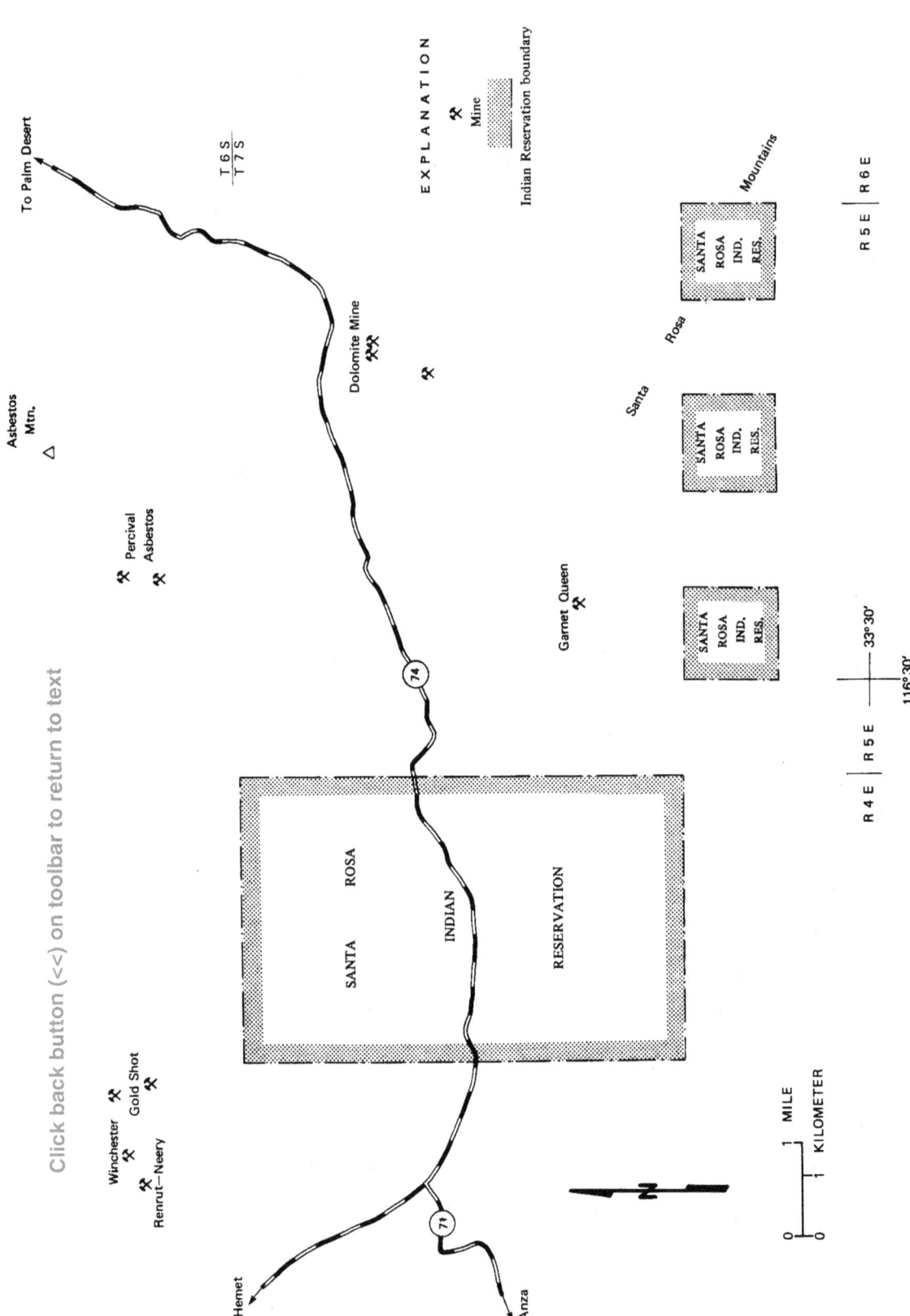

Click back button (<<) on toolbar to return to text

Figure 39. Mineral resource map of the Santa Rosa Indian Reservation.

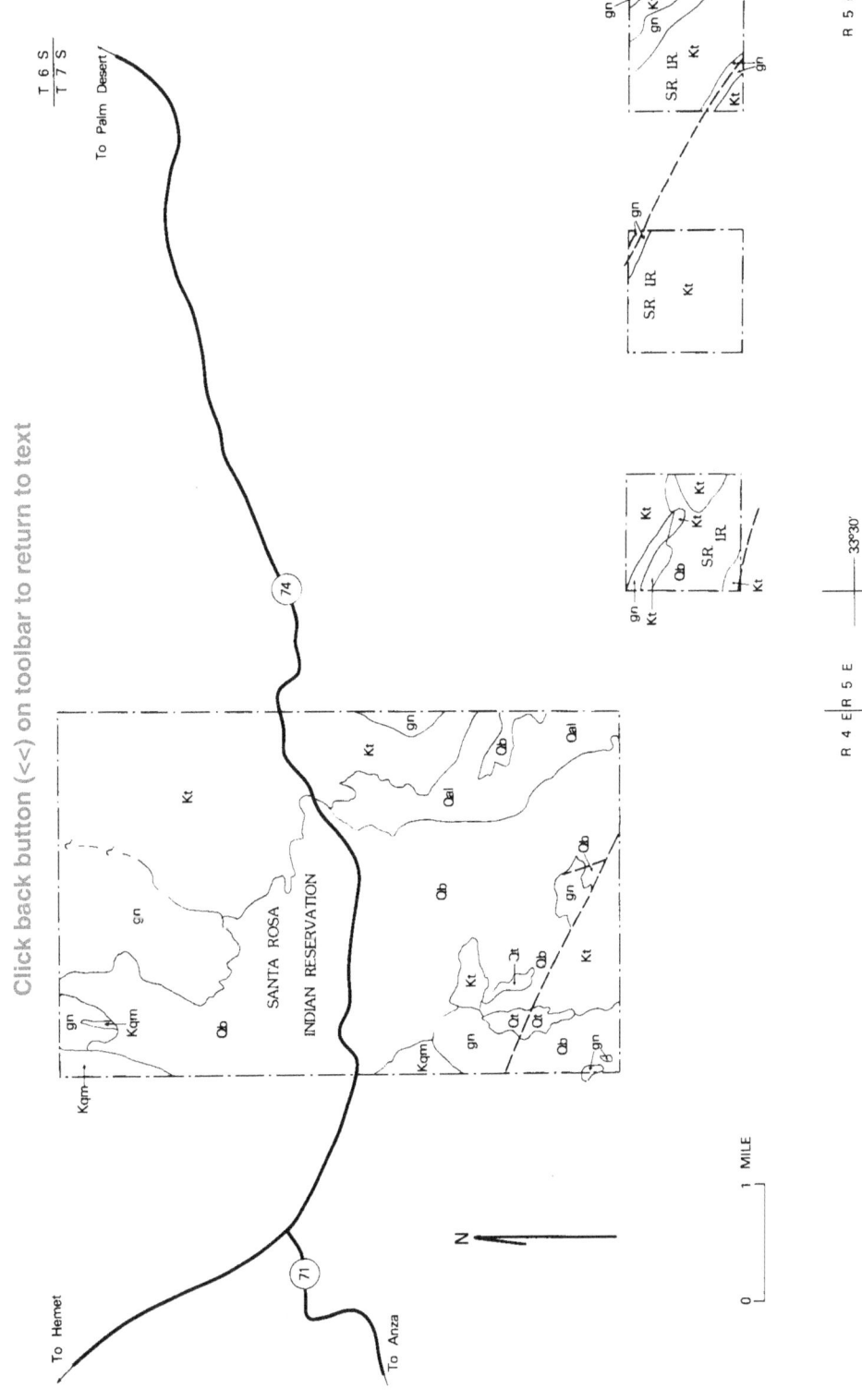

Figure 40. Geologic map of part of the Santa Rosa Indian Reservation (Wright, 1946; Sharp, 1967). Bautista beds (Qb); tonalite (Kt); schist and gneiss (gn).

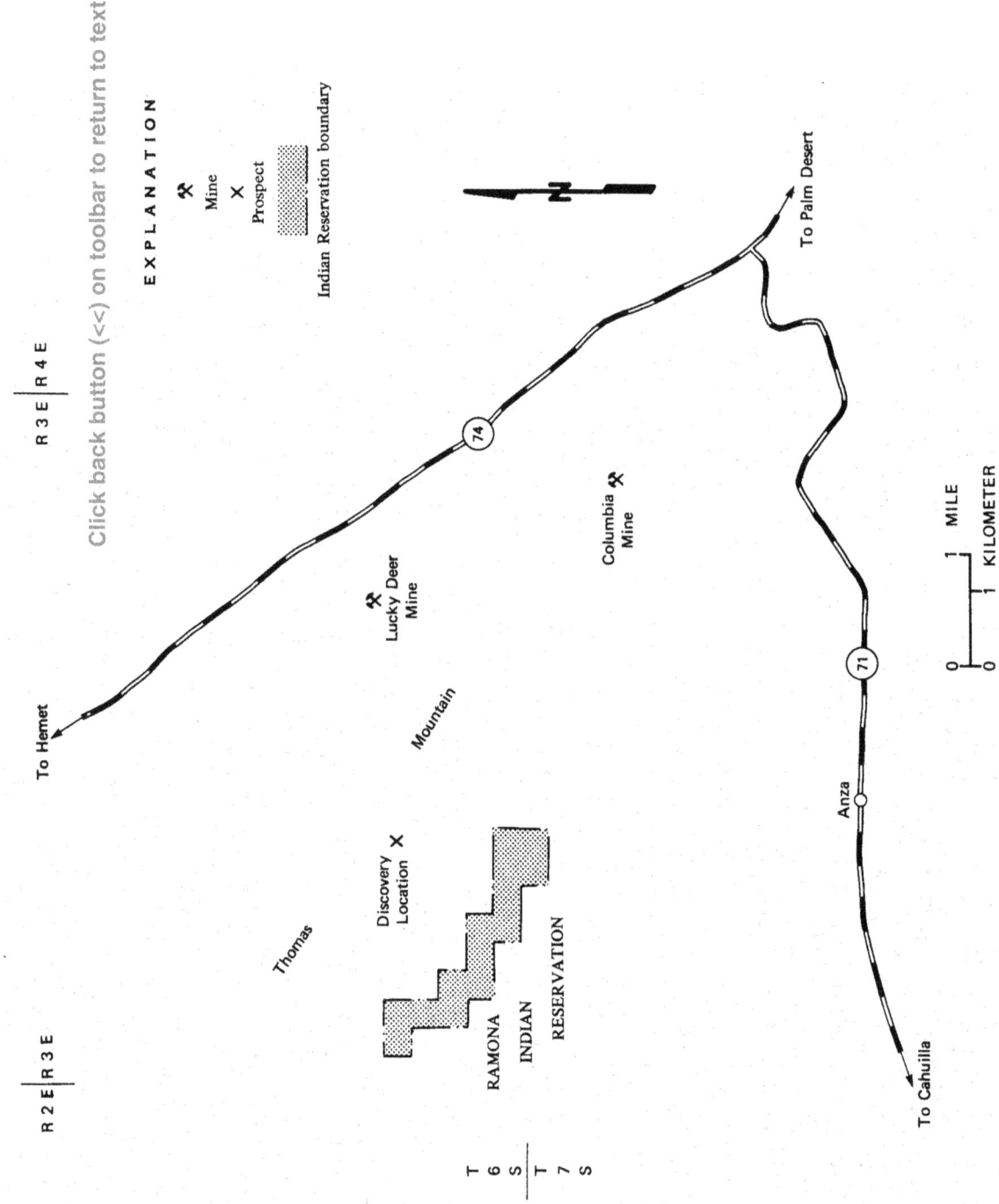

Click back button (<<) on toolbar to return to text

Figure 41. Mineral resource map of the Ramona Indian Reservation.

Click back button (<<) on toolbar to return to text

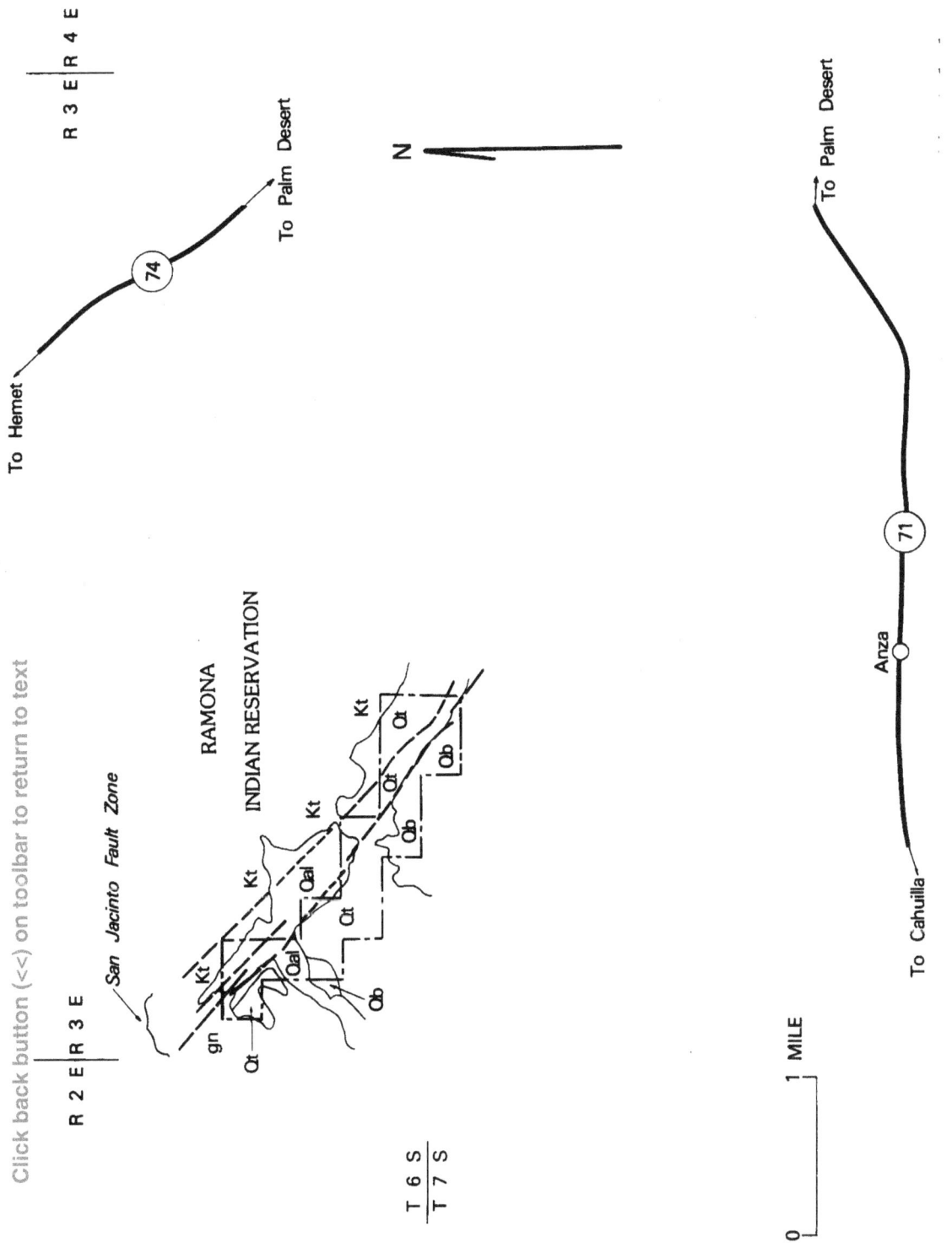

Figure 42. Geology of the Ramona Indian Reservation (from Sharp, 1967). Quaternary alluvial deposits (Qal); terrace deposits (Qt); Bautista beds (Qb); tonalite (Kt); gneiss (gn).

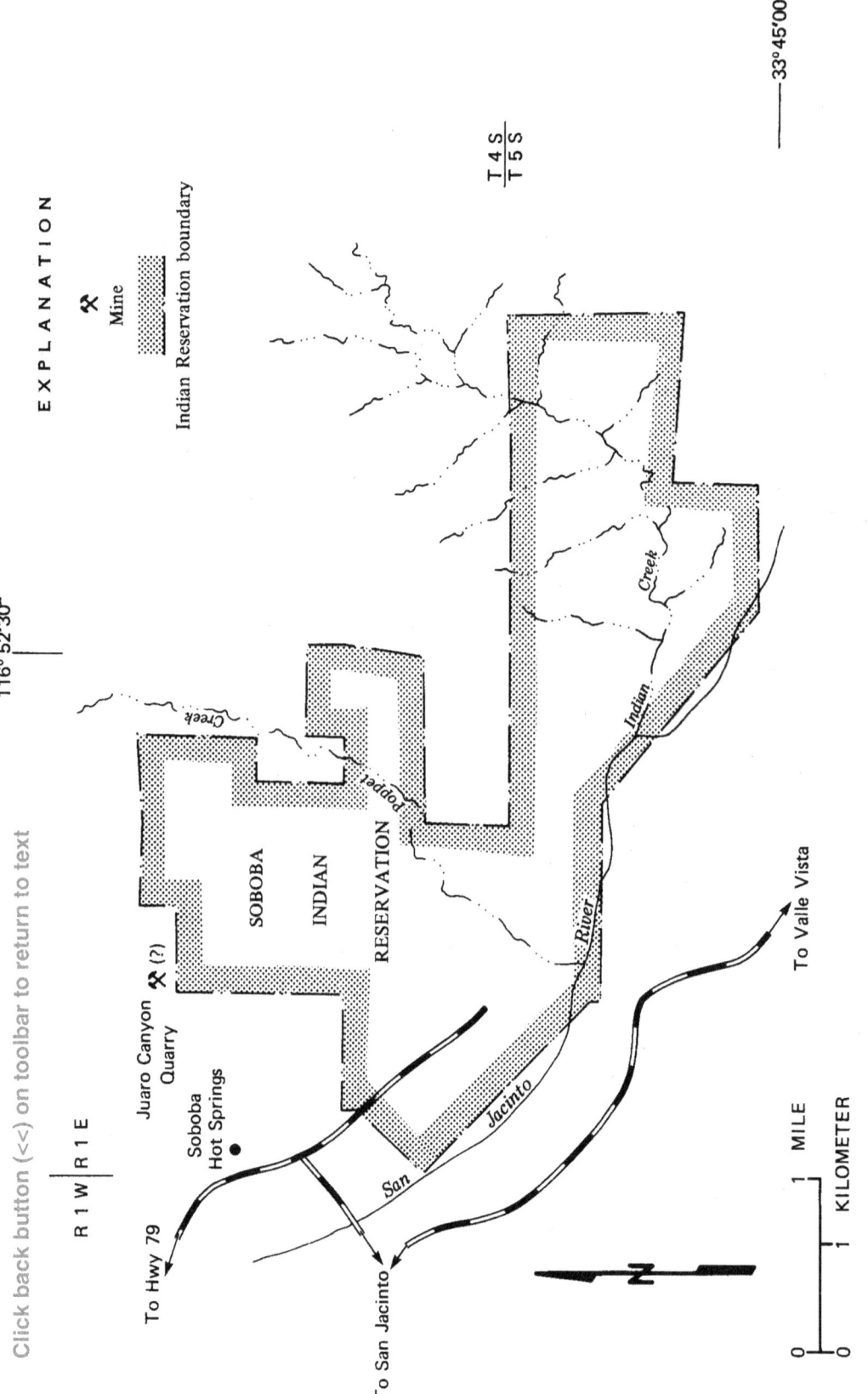

Click back button (<<) on toolbar to return to text

EXPLANATION

⚒

Mine

Indian Reservation boundary

116° 52'30"

R 1 W | R 1 E

Juaro Canyon
Quarry ⚒ (?)

Soboba
Hot Springs ●

To Hwy 79

SOBOBA

INDIAN

RESERVATION

Poppet Creek

Creek

River

San Jacinto

Indian

To San Jacinto

To Valle Vista

T 4 S
――――
T 5 S

33° 45'00"

N

0   1   MILE
0   1   KILOMETER

Figure 43. Mineral resource map of the Soboba Indian Reservation.

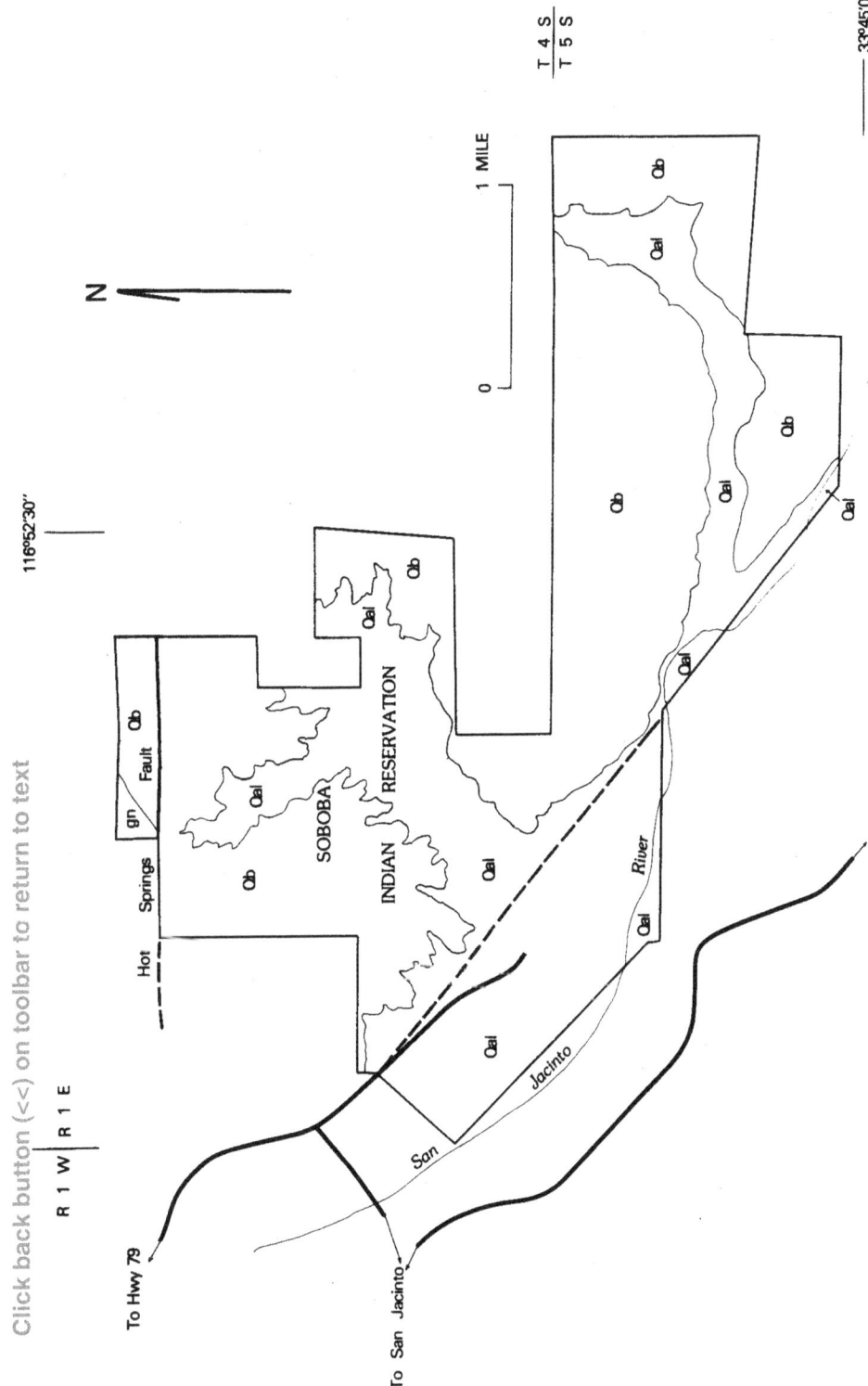

Figure 44. Geologic map of the Soboba Indian Reservation (from Fraser, 1931). Quaternary alluvial deposits (Qal); Bautista beds (Qb); gneiss (gn).

Click back button (<<) on toolbar to return to text

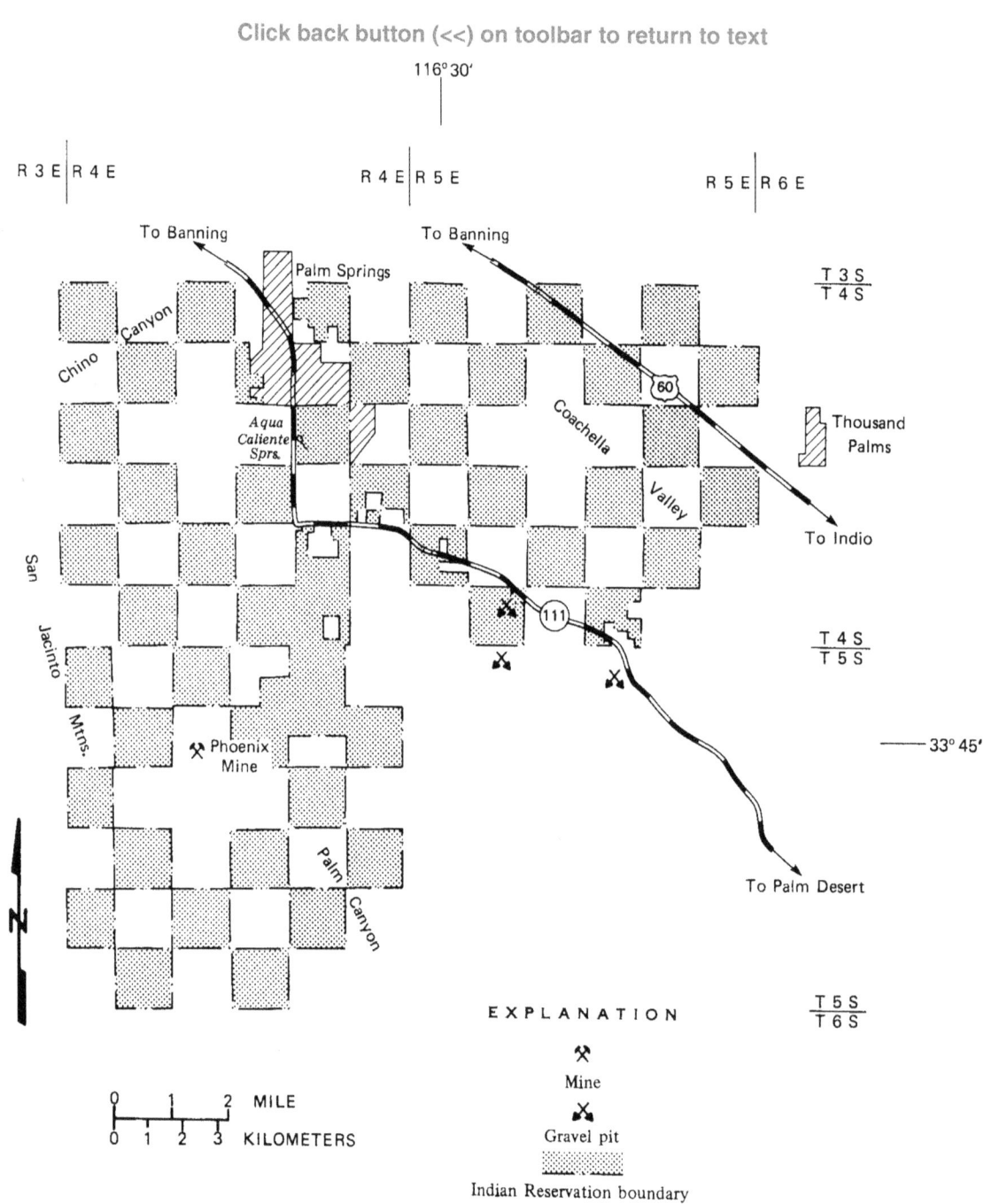

Figure 45. Mineral resource map of the Agua Caliente Indian Reservation.

Click back button (<<) on toolbar to return to text

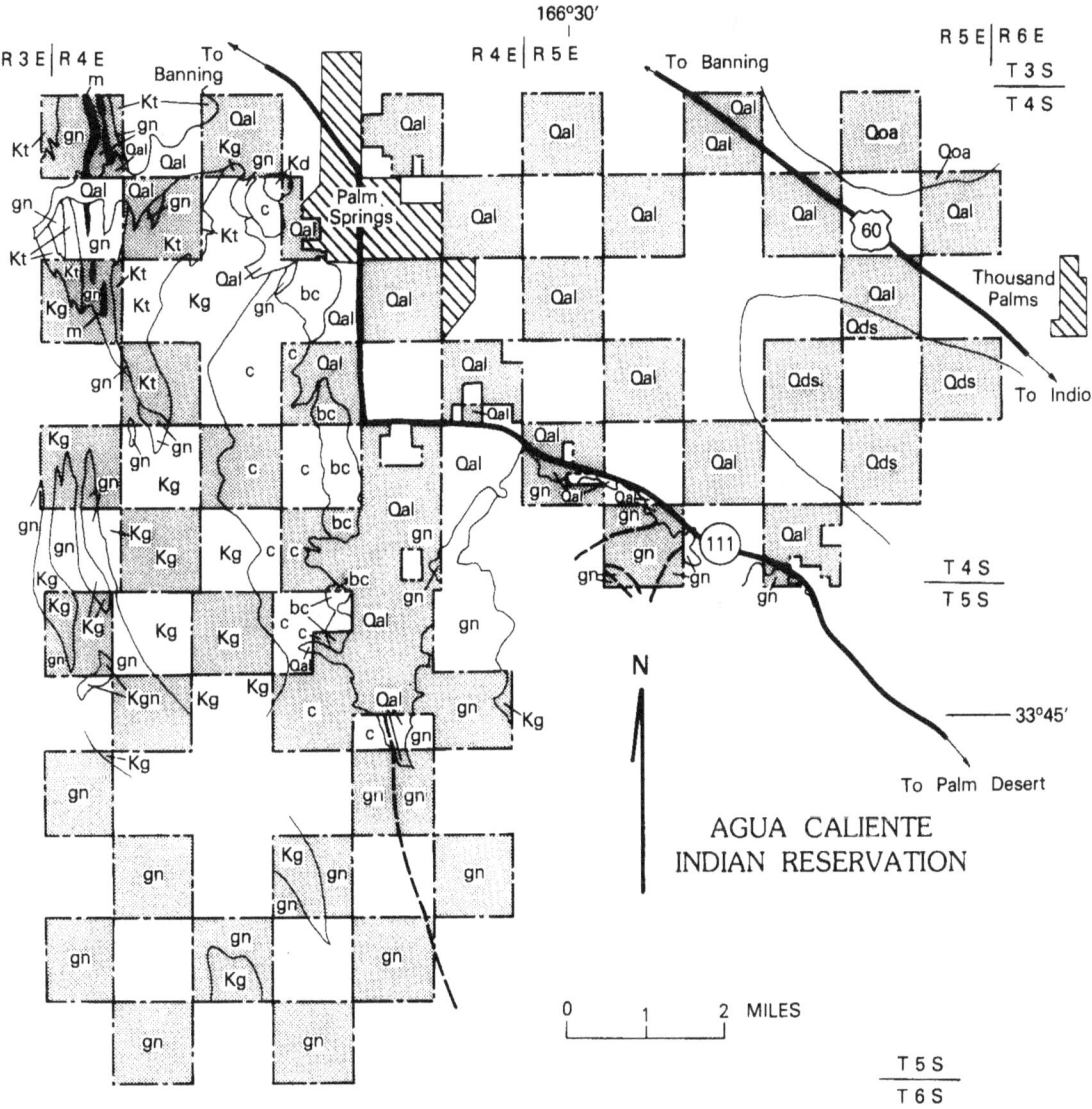

Figure 46. Geologic map of the Agua Caliente Indian Reservation (from Dibblee, U.S. Geologic Survey unpublished mapping, 1971; Rogers, 1965). Quaternary alluvial deposits (Qal); dune sand (Qds); older alluvial deposits (Qoa); granodiorite (Kg); tonalite (Kt); schist and gneiss (gn); marble (m); cataclastic rock (c); biotite-rich cataclastic rock (bc).

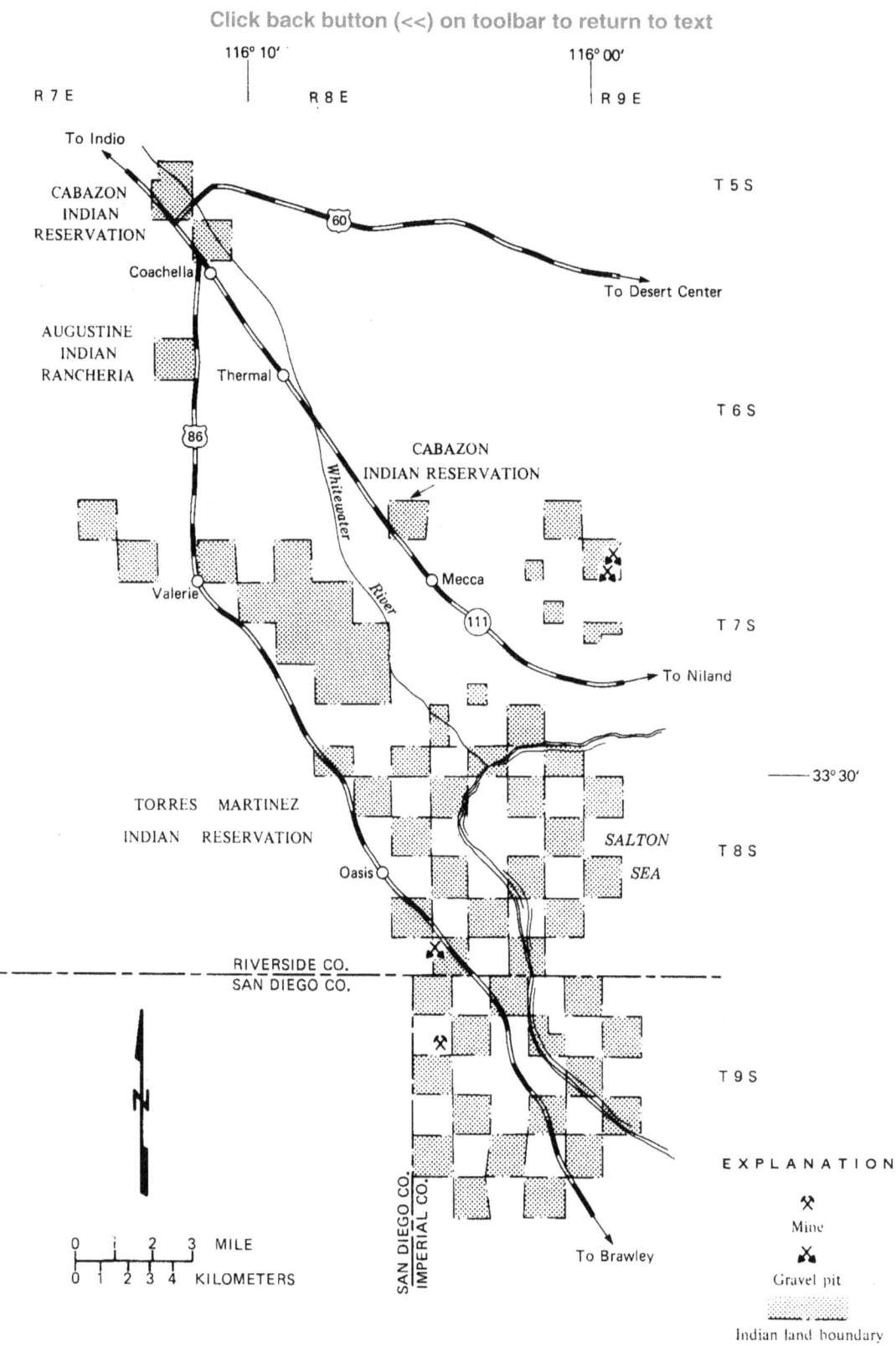

Figure 47. Mineral resource map of the Torres Martinez and Cabazon Indian Reservations and Augustine Indian Rancheria.

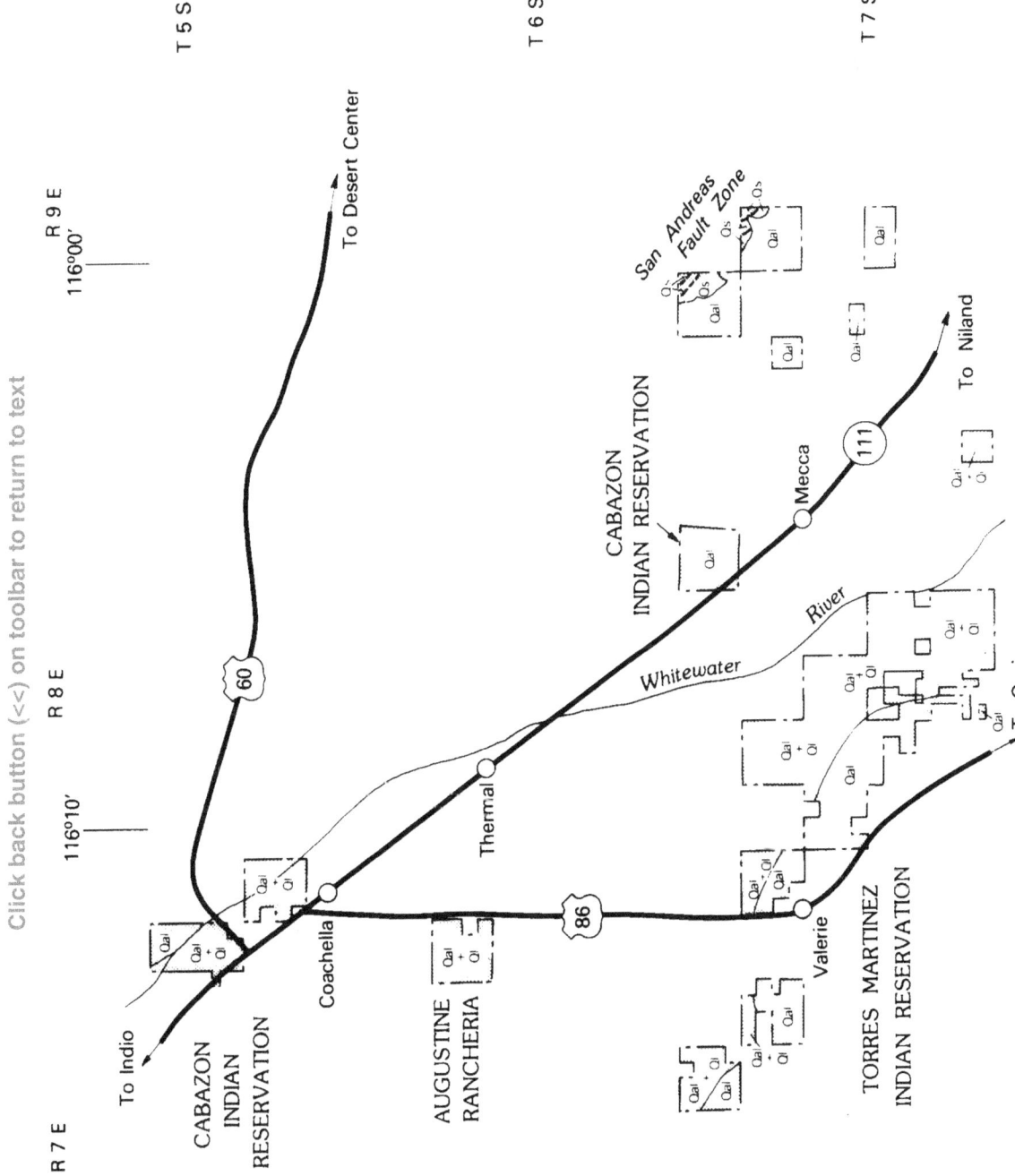

Figure 48. Geologic map of the Cabezon Indian Reservation and Augustine Indian Rancheria (from Rogers, 1965). Quaternary alluvial deposits (Qal); Quaternary lake deposits (Ql).

Click back button (<<) on toolbar to return to text

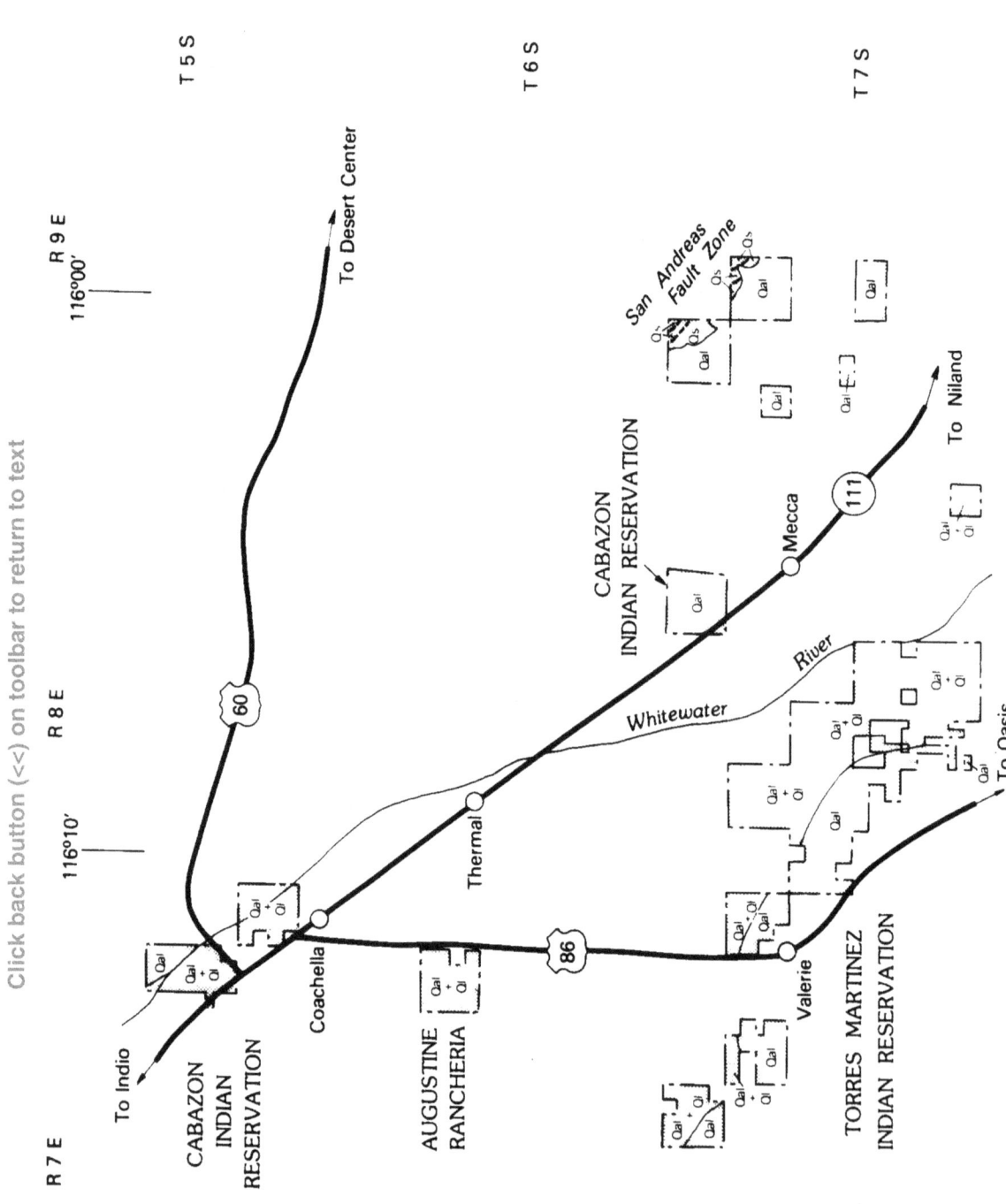

Figure 49. Geologic map of part of the Torres Martinez Indian Reservation (from Rogers, 1965). Quaternary alluvial deposits (Qal); Quaternary terrace (Qt); Quaternary dune sand (Qds); Pliocene nonmarine sediments (Ts); Pliocene marine sediments (Tsm); Pliocene volcanics (Tv); granitic rock (Kg); schist and gneiss (gn); marble (m).

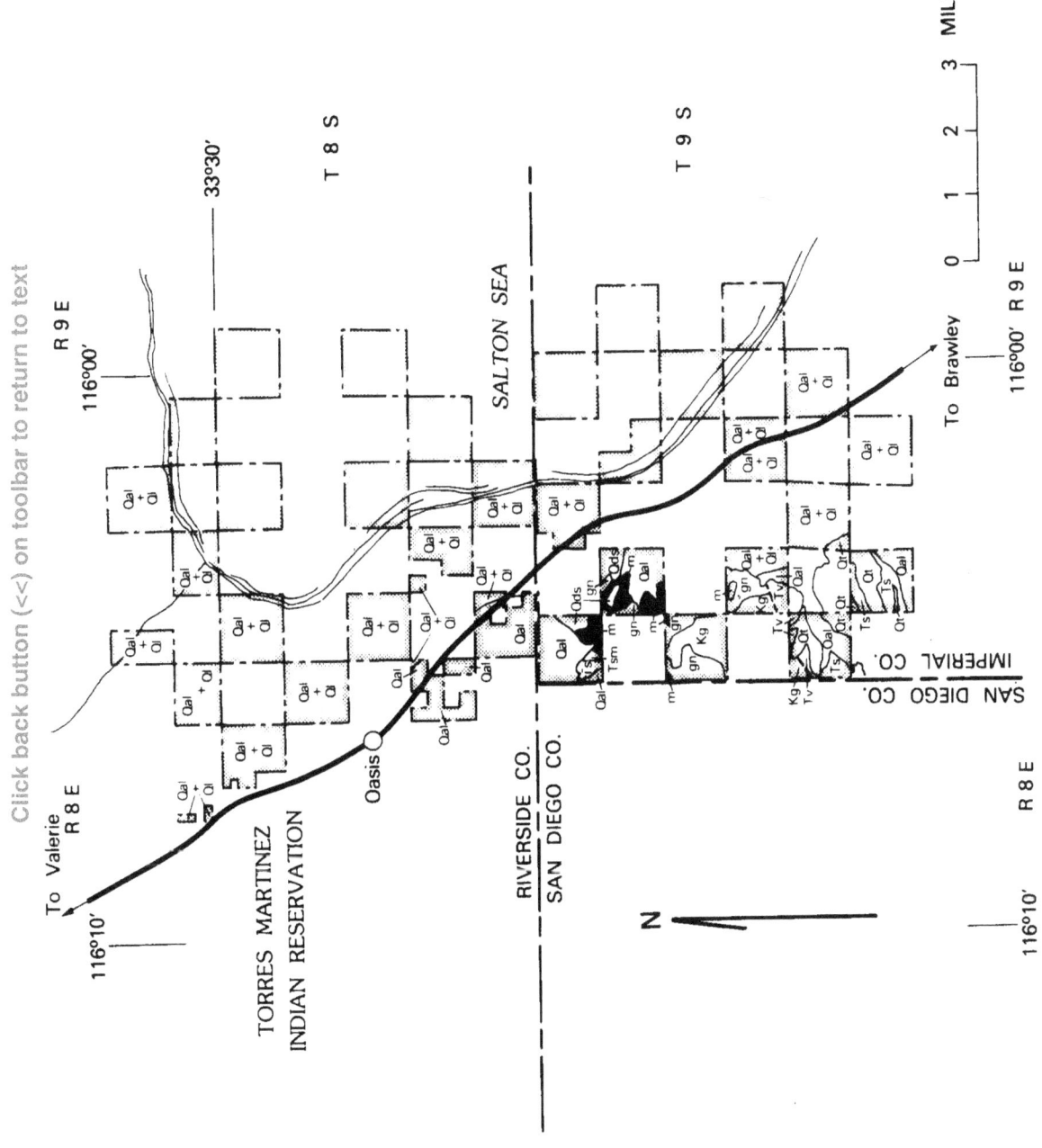

Figure 50. Geologic map of part of the Torres Martinez Indian Reservation (from Rogers, 1965). Quarternary alluvial deposits (Qal); Quarternary lake deposits (Ql); Pleistocene sediments (Qs).

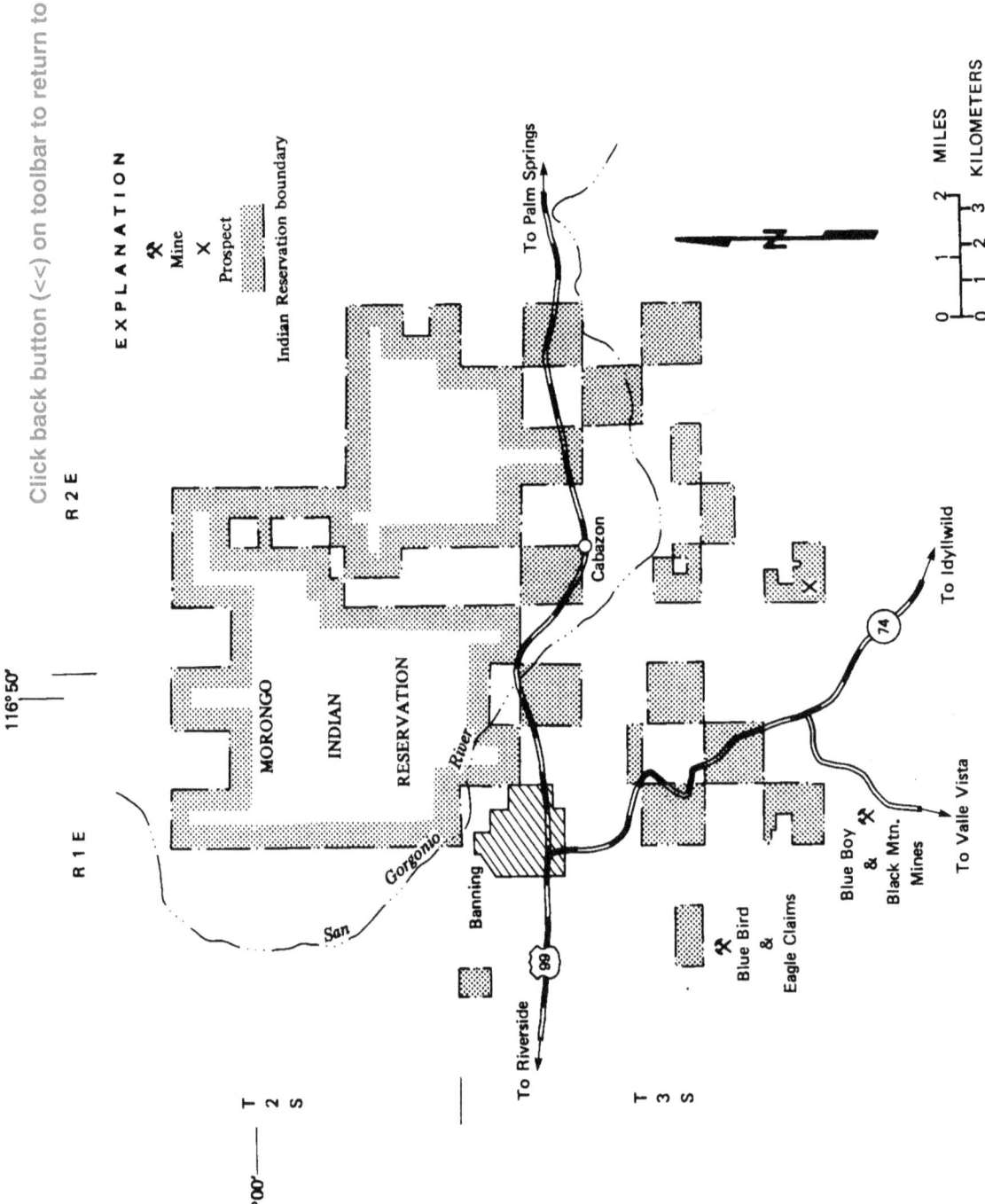

Figure 51. Mineral resource map of the Morongo Indian Reservation.

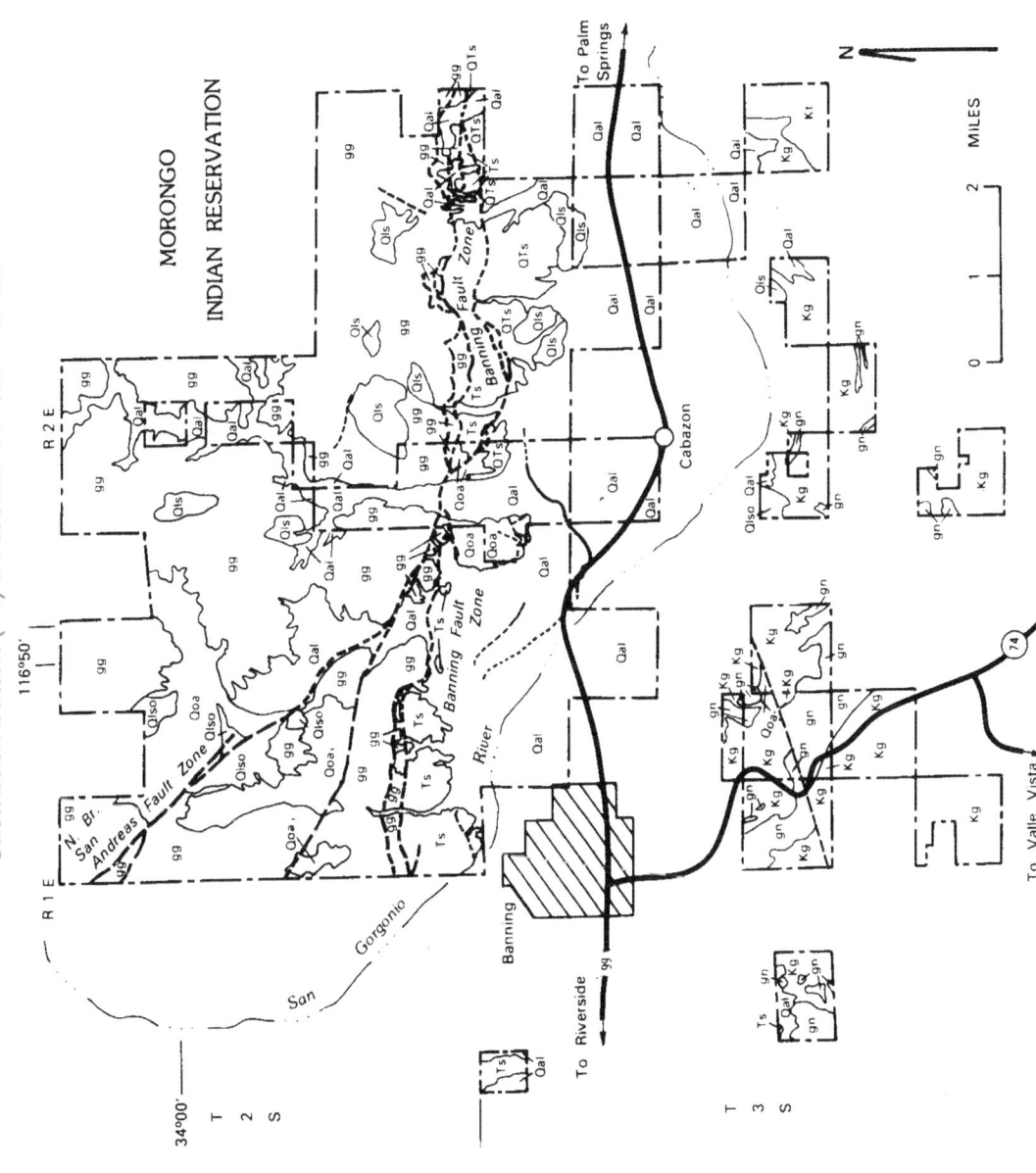

Figure 52. Geologic map of part of the Morongo Indian Reservation (from Allen, 1931; U.S. Geological Survey unpublished mapping). Younger alluvium (Qal); younger landslides (Qls); older landslides (Qlso); older alluvium (Qoa); older alluvial terrace deposits (Qoa); Cabezon Conglomerate (QTs); Tertiary sediments and volcanics (Hathaway Formation, Imperial Formation, and Painted Hills Formation) (Ts); San Timoteo Formation (Tst); undifferentiated granitic rocks (Kg); sphene-bearing tonalite (Kt); schist and gneiss (gn); mixed schist, gneiss, and granitic rocks (gg).

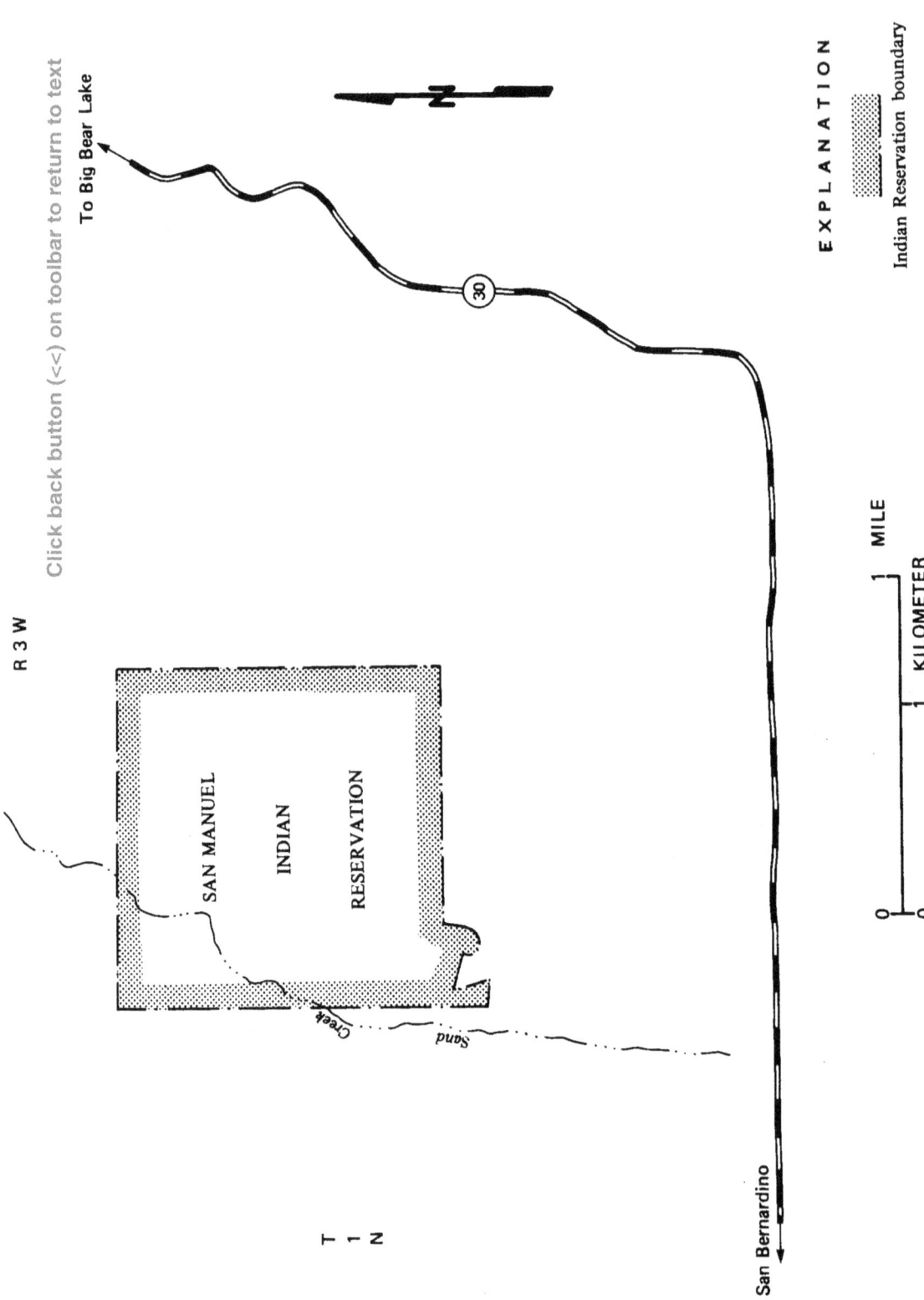

Figure 53. Mineral resource map of the San Manuel Indian Reservation.

Click back button (<<) on toolbar to return to text

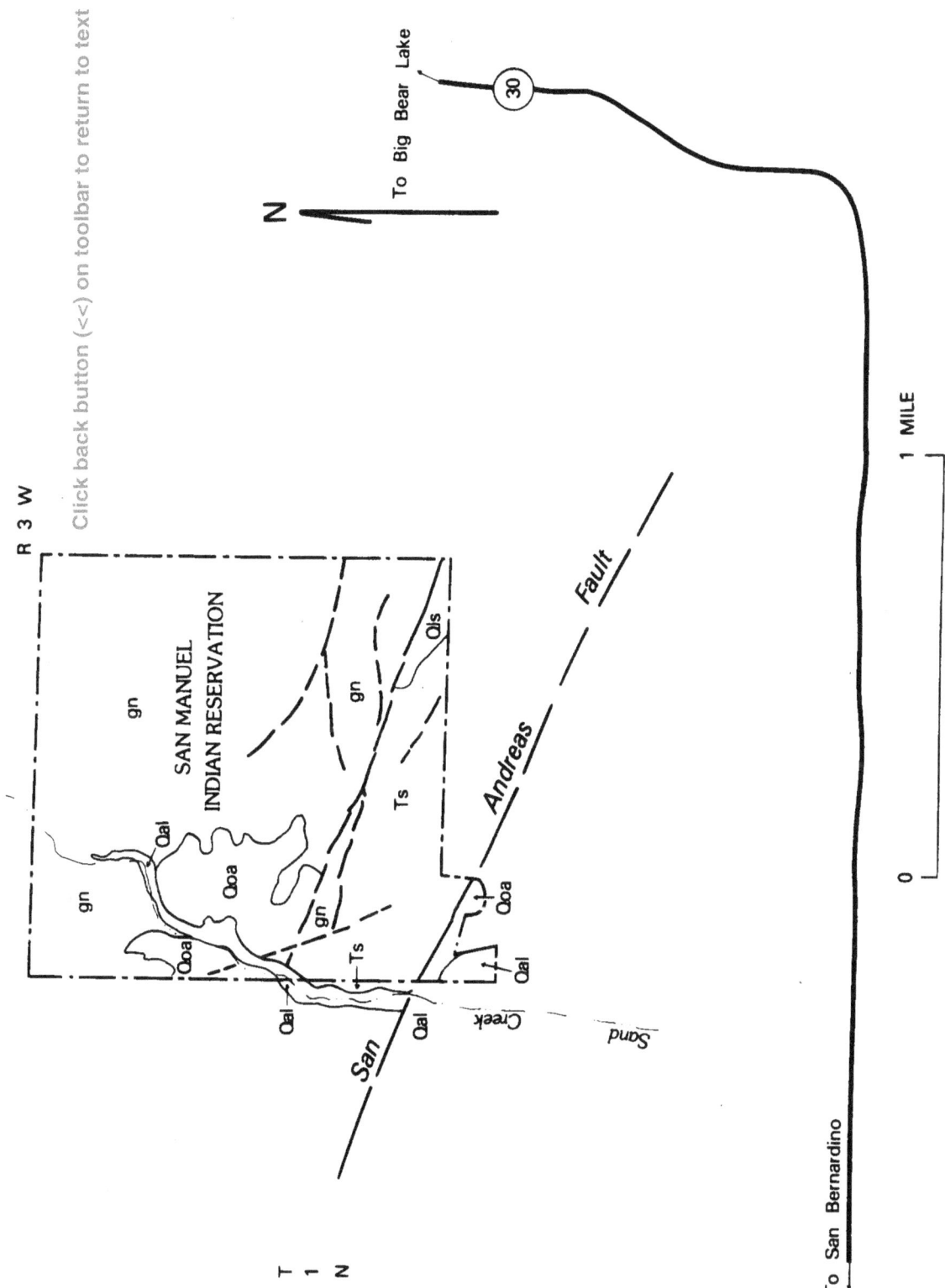

Figure 54. Geologic map of the San Manuel Indian Reservation (from Miller, unpublished U.S. Geological Survey mapping). Quaternary alluvial deposits (Qal); older Quaternary alluvial deposits (Qoa); Older landslide deposits (Qls); Tertiary sediments (Ts);gneiss (gn).

Click back button (<<) on toolbar to return to text

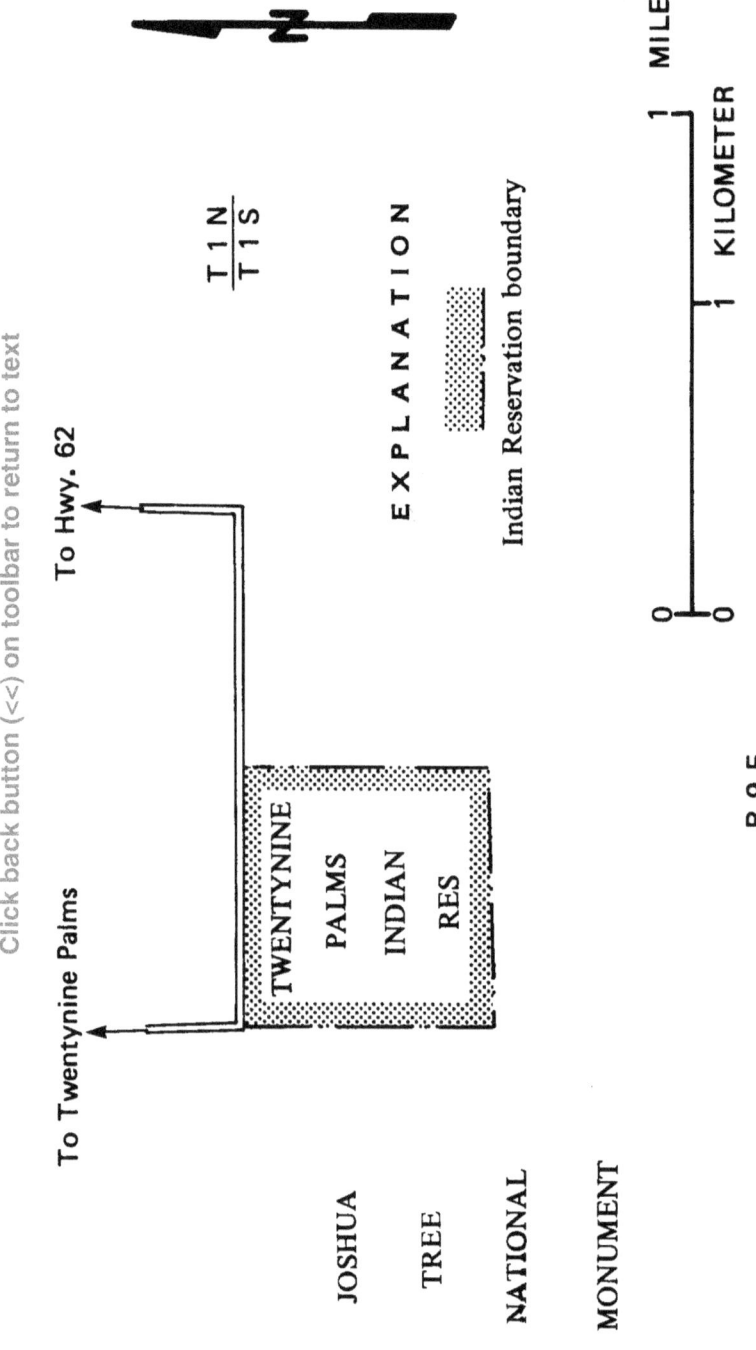

Figure 55. Location map of the Twentynine Palms Indian Reservation.

Click back button (<<) on toolbar to return to text

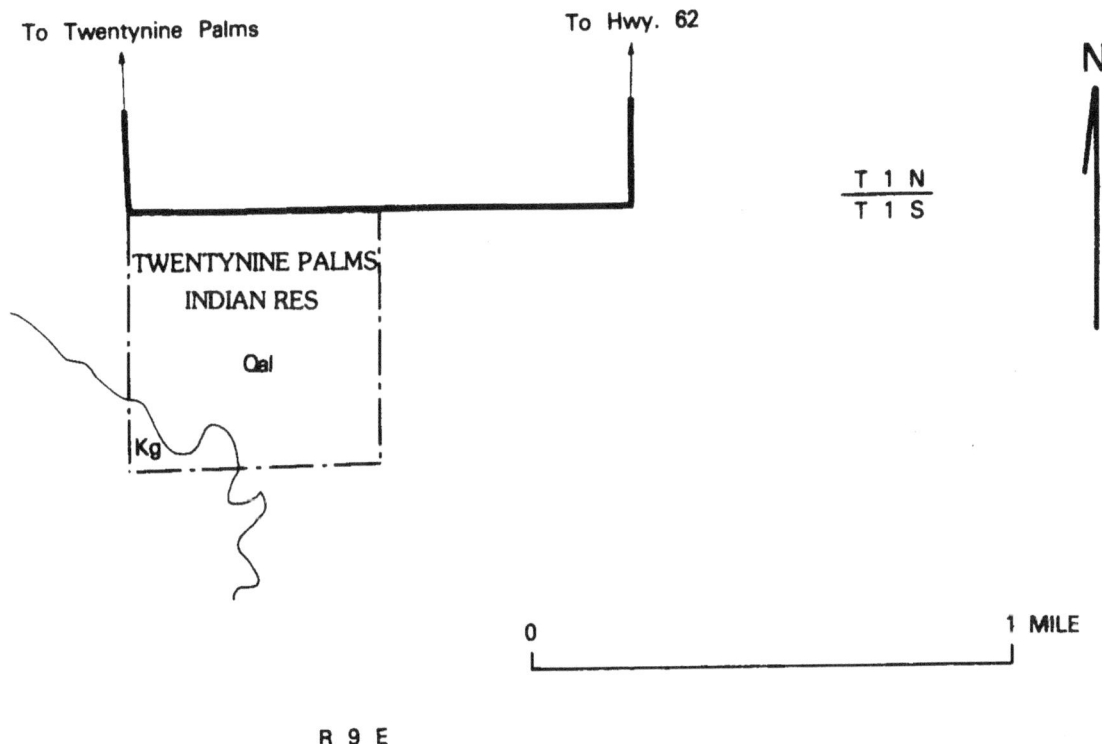

Figure 56. Geologic map of the Twentynine Palms Indian Reservation (from Rogers, 1967). Quaternary alluvial deposits (Qal); quartz monzonite (Kg).

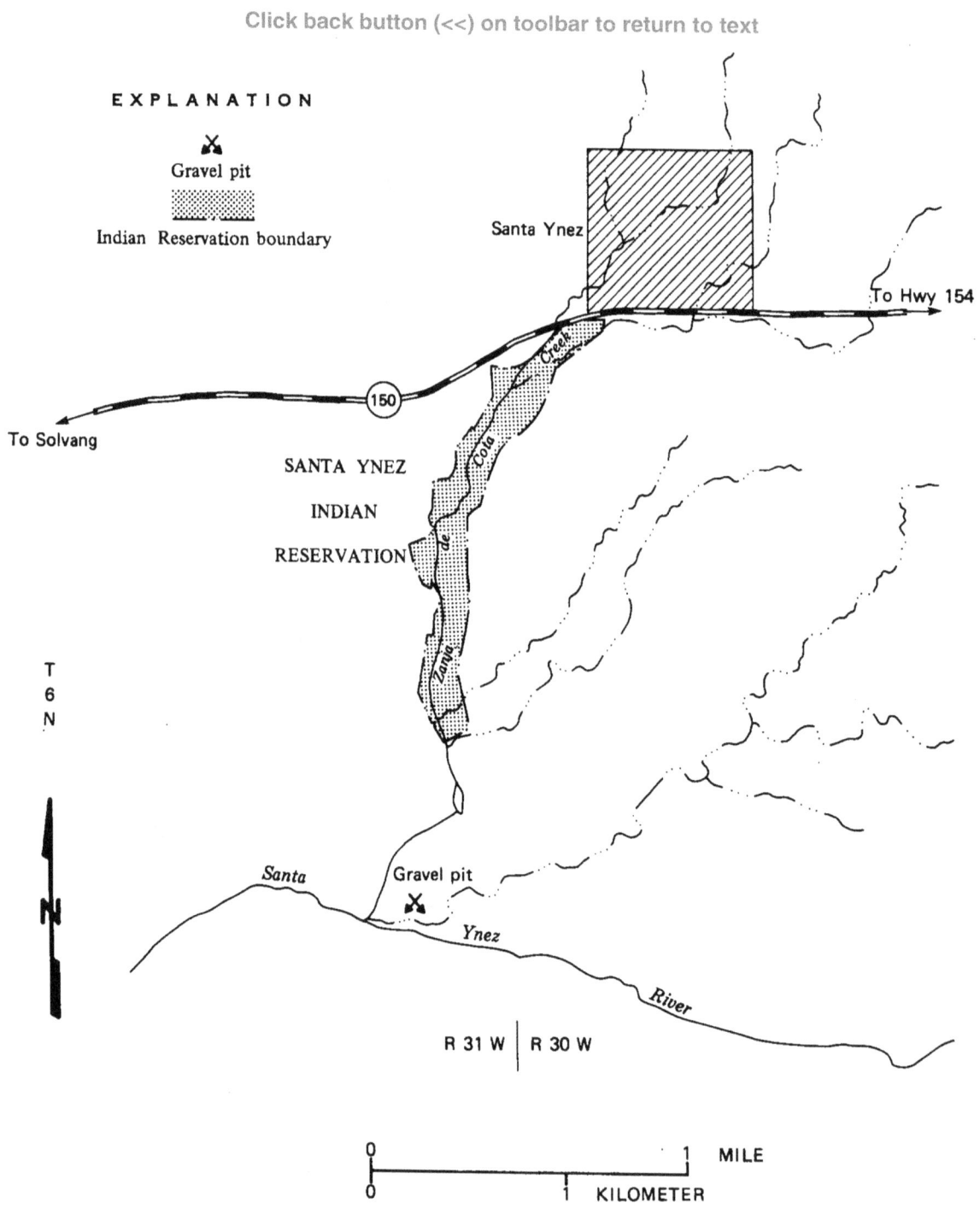

Figure 57. Mineral resource map of the Santa Ynez Indian Reservation.